# THE GREATEST
## JEWISH CITY
# IN THE WORLD

# THE GREATEST
# JEWISH CITY
# IN THE WORLD

by HARRY GOLDEN

Selected photographs by Jay Maisel

DOUBLEDAY & COMPANY, INC., Garden City, New York
1972

ISBN: 0–385–00760–4
Library of Congress Catalog Card Number 74–166422
Copyright © 1972 by Harry Golden
Photographs copyright © 1972 by J. Maisel
All Rights Reserved
Printed in the United States of America
First Edition

PICTURE CREDITS:

All of the color photographs reproduced in this book were taken by Jay Maisel.

Amalgamated Clothing Workers of America: Page 145B
American Jewish Congress: Page 201
American Society of Composers, Authors, and Publishers: Pages 41T, 41B, 91T 92, 93T, 93B
The Bettmann Archive, Inc.: Pages 35, 51, 82, 91B, 108, 140, 164, 177, 187B, 188, 189
Peder Björkegren: Page 214B
Black Star: Page 66 (Photograph by Ray Schorr); Page 111 (Photograph by Flip Schulke)
Harold Blumenfeld: Page 125
Collection of George Eastman House: Pages 54, 101, 136, 137
The Hall of Fame for Great Americans at New York University: Page 49
Herbert Halweil: Page 171
International Ladies' Garment Workers' Union: Pages 138, 141
The *Jewish Daily Forward:* Page 180.
Jewish Labor Committee: Pages 139, 145T
Karsh: Page 161
Richard Lescsak: Page 212
The Library of Congress: Page 79

Dedicated to the memory of
Dr. David de Sola Pool,
a great rabbi and a great friend.

# Acknowledgments

No BOOK of this sort has even been written without the assistance of other books and informed individuals. I take this opportunity to acknowledge my indebtedness. I hold none of them responsible for errors of fact or judgment, if any, that appear in the following pages.

The *Jewish Chronicle* of London, where a similar, shorter essay, "The Greatest Jewish City in the World," first appeared.

Nathaniel Weyl's *The Creative Elite in America* (Public Affairs Press, Washington, D.C., 1966) was particularly helpful. M. R. Werner's *Tammany Hall* (Doubleday, Doran, N.Y., 1928) provided data for part of Chapter 4, as well as Irving Howe's article in *Midstream* (January 1968) "The Lower East Side," for Chapter 6. *Jewish Tourist's guide to the United States* by Bernard Postal and Lionel Koppman (Jewish Publication Society of America, Philadelphia, 1954) contributed to the information found in parts of Chapters 7 and 8. *The American Gospel of Success: Individualism and Beyond* (Quadrangle Books, Chicago, 1965) by Moses Richin helped with Chapters 8 and 9. For data on Macy's and Ohrbach's in Chapter 9, I am indebted to *The Great Merchants* by Tom Mahoney and Leonard Sloan (Harper & Row, N.Y., 1966).

*Playboy* for October 1970 provided the feature on Lainie Kazan in Chapter 9. Some of the material in Chapter 6 is based on Ann Geracimo's article "Games Children Play in New York City," published in *New York* magazine. I drew upon the same periodical for information on "Restricted Co-Ops: The Gentlemen's Agreement" by Nicholas Pilleggi. Parts of Chapter 8 depended upon Gus Tyler's article, "The Legacy of the Jewish Labor Movement," *The Jewish Digest* for September 1970 (originally published in *Midstream*).

Sources for Chapter 12 include, among other items, Frederick Lewis Allen's *Only Yesterday* (Harper & Row, N.Y., 1931); pamphlets and newspaper clippings preserved in the files of the Anti-Defamation League; Nathaniel Weyl's book, *The Jew in American Politics* (Arlington House, New Rochelle, 1968); and Kenneth Braiterman's article, "The Jewish Defence League: What Safety in Karate?" from *Midstream* for April, 1970.

In addition to these sources, I used many others not mentioned here, but noted in the text.

People in New York City and elsewhere contributed to this volume. Among these are in particular Irving Shulman; Bernard Warach at the Jewish Association for Services for the Aged; Oscar Cohen; Dore Schary of the Anti-Defamation League; Richard Blumberg, Al Goldstein, Abel Green; Irving M. Engel, Bert Gold, and Judith Hershlag Muffs of the American Jewish Committee; Carol Horn of the National Federation of Temple Youth; Philip Goldman of the Bronx High School of Science; officials and clergy of Temple Emanu-El; Tamar de Sola Pool, widow of the rabbi Dr. David de Sola Pool; and many other persons who generously gave of their time and special knowledge.

My son Billy, more formally, Professor William Goldhurst of the Humanities Department of the University of Florida, assisted in the research and editing of this book.

# Contents

# THE GREATEST
## JEWISH CITY
# IN THE WORLD

# The Greeks, the Romans, and the Jews

THE THREE great cities of history were all in the Mediterranean area: Athens, Rome, and Jerusalem. There isn't a city in the western world today which could accommodate the twentieth century were it not for the gifts these first three bestowed upon us.

The Athenians not only invented democracy but gave us art, philosophy, and the idea of school education. The Greeks invented the theater, the Lyceum, and the Academy. Had they not lost a vast and corrupting land war with Sparta, they might have succeeded in civilizing the rest of the known world. They had beaten the Persians at Marathon when they let Darius overextend his lines of supply and they had beaten his son Xerxes in the sea battle at Salamis when they boxed in his fleet. Then they committed the same tactical mistakes themselves against Sparta and left the peninsula to the Macedonians, Philip first and then his son, Alexander.

The Romans gave us law. They developed the concept of municipal government. They had mayors, councillors, senators, and the idea of self-perpetuating civil machinery. The Romans published the first *Congressional Record*, calling it the *Daily Doings of the Senate*.

The Jews of Jerusalem made the concept of the individual a meaningful one. They did not consign the old and infirm to savage exile outside the gates of the city but made it the law that they live within. The Jews were the first people in history to publish casualty lists and the first to insist that one day—the Sabbath—belonged jointly to the individual and God.

The citizens of these three cities, of course, had other virtues and skills. The Romans were supreme engineers, the Greeks marvelous merchants, and the Jews great scholars. But it was their contribution of paideia, the law, and the majesty of the individual which most influenced citizens in other places and in other times.

The one modern city which has bequeathed a tradition equal to these ancient three is New York. What New York City did was to accept an immigrant population, turn it into a citizen population, and do so within a generation. Rome made the inhabitants of every conquered territory *cives Romani*—to no avail against the Vandals. The Greeks were xenophobes, distrustful of the stranger and the Jews of Judea were literally zealots about their way of life.

New York was the first city to announce it had room for everyone and the first city to prove the truth of its own announcement. Other cities in the world have had schools and law and humanitarian concern, but New York best combines these offerings for foreigners, immigrants, and the children of adventurers.

While this book is devoted to the Jewish community of the City of New York, it goes beyond that. The Jewish community of New York is really a microcosm of Jewish America, representing the three waves of immigration that washed over our shores: the Sephardic Jews from England and Holland in colonial times; the German Jews after 1848; and the vast immigration from Eastern Europe—Russia, Poland, Romania, Hungary, and Austria—from 1880 to 1920. Here in New York we have the story of all the Jews of America, the heartbreaking comic and tragic struggles between the very old and the very new, in many matters all at once: religion, clothes, manners, language, culture.

The late nineteenth-century Jewish emigration to New York from Eastern Europe created the Jewish community of America. At the end of the Revolutionary War there were over three thousand religious establishments in the county, five of which were Jewish—in Newport, Rhode Island, New York City, Philadelphia, Charleston, South Carolina, and Savannah, Georgia. In all of America there weren't three thousand Jews, barely 1 per cent of the population. By the end of the Civil War, there were one hundred and fifty thousand Jews in the United States. Then the nation numbered twenty-three million. But at the end of World War I, there were more than two million Jews living here, in the main immigrants from Eastern Europe. They established the fraternities, the philanthropies, the social action societies and the labor unions. The Roosevelt New Deal contained many of the principles brought by the Jews to America from the Pale of Settlements and ghettoes of Europe: Bury the dead and take care of the widows and orphans; and if a man is sick he needs a doctor and if he's unemployed, he needs a check. These benefits were provided by the fraternity to which he belonged and to which he paid monthly dues.

The earliest of these organizations was the Bialystoker Mutual Aid Society. By 1890 there were thirty-one major Eastern European societies and dozens of smaller *Vereins* providing small loans and paying funeral "benefits." By 1905 most of these *Vereins* had established systems of unemployment and health insurance. The *Vereins*, in the main, were organized on the basis of point of origin in Europe, and they were known as *Landsmannschäften*. For example: my family came from the town of Mikulincze in the Galician province of the Austro-Hungarian Empire, and we belonged to the *Mikulinczer Verein*.

Another of these great self-help organizations was the Hebrew Free Loan Society on New York's Lower East Side. It was founded in 1892 on a capital investment of ninety-five dollars. It granted loans of up to five hundred dollars without interest to needy people, employed or unemployed, and made these loans without an investigation or a demand for collateral. It only required the endorsement of two responsible persons who had bank accounts or who did business in Greater New York.

The borrower had to promise to repay his loan within ten months. The Hebrew Free Loan Society has had a fantastic record of repayments. In its seventy-three year history it has seen forty-five million dollars lent to eight hundred thousand borrowers. Though the Jews on the Lower East Side lived amid grinding poverty, they were proud that they depended neither on city nor private charity, but were able to make do on their own.

There was even a "Marshall Plan" in New York's ghetto over sixty years ago. Nearly every home had a blue and white box nailed to the wall in which we dropped a penny or two every day. It was for the Jewish National Fund, to buy land from the Arabs. Once a month an elderly woman came to the tenement flats to empty the boxes and to indulge in the important ritual of "a glass of tea." This was protocol. Each of the families she visited would have lost face if she had declined the invitation. On collection day the National Fund woman drank fifty glasses of tea.

There are many other things to be said about Jews and about New York as a Jewish city beyond what I shall here attempt. I only hope that this book will inspire others to say them, if what they say is wise, tolerant, or helpful. My book does not pretend to be definitive, except in love of its subject, situation, and site.

# CHAPTER 1

# The Greatest Jewish City
# in the World

WITHIN ITS LIMITS, New York City has more Jews than have ever congregated in a single city in the history of the world. The mass of Jewish immigration from Eastern Europe, especially from Russia, Poland, Romania, and Austria-Hungary has been the salient fact in the creation of this unprecedented concentration. Between 1880 and the final passage of the Reed-Johnson Restrictive Immigration Bill in 1920 more than two million Jews fleeing from pogroms, revolutions, or economic, political, and social disabilities arrived in the United States. Whole families of Jews came to New York, often entire communities. Few of them went any further: in the big city they found other Jews who shared their religious traditions and customs, friends and family who helped these greenhorns gain a foothold in the New World.

Two previous waves of Jewish immigration had washed into the United States: Spanish and Portuguese Jews came by way of Amsterdam and London in colonial times, and a larger wave of German Jews followed after the revolution in Central Europe in 1848.

Yet why would a large majority of sophisticated Americans call New York a Jewish City yet still call Boston, for example, The Hub instead of an Irish city?

Proportionately, there are probably as many Irishmen in Boston as there are Jews in New York. Which is to say that neither constitutes a majority of the population but that both have invested the respective cities with certain characteristics.

In Boston, the Irish have had, in fact, far more success than the Jews in New York. The Irish are politically sophisticated and have done better politically even in New York than the Jews although they are fewer in number.

Still, we say New York is a Jewish City and it isn't because you don't have to be Jewish to like Levy's rye bread. The Irish came by steerage to Boston because it was $9.00 cheaper than steerage to New York. New York was the nearest immigration center from Bremen, Germany, for the immigrating Jews.

Some of the Jews moved on to Philadelphia and to Chicago, even to Atlanta, but 90 per cent remained in New York because they had no money to venture further west. They funneled into one area of the city, the Lower East Side, filling the six-story tenements with children, parents, uncles, aunts, and boarders.

The Jews, alone of the immigrant groups, did to New York what the Irish never did to Boston: the Jews virtually transformed the city.

The invention of ready-made clothes was an American innovation. About the time of the mass Jewish immigration, manufacturers realized that clothing was a seasonal product and that maintaining a factory year round ate up profits. So the manufacturers moved the factories into the homes, a system described as the "sweatshop system," the most ingenious process ever devised for overexertion. The cheapest labor was provided by these immigrant Jews, who, destitute and unfamiliar with the English language and the American mores, had little other choice. By 1890 the garment industry, which had once been populated by the English, the Germans, and some Irish, was now almost wholly populated by Jewish workers turning out shirts, suits, pants, and coats in their tenements and small lofts.

These immigrant Jews from Russia and Poland were Orthodox Jews, observing all the religious prescriptions no matter how arcane and all the dietary laws no matter how inconvenient. Because they would eat only kosher meat, New York remained an important slaughtering center long after other American cities were content to buy beef from Chicago. The Jews by diverse and imaginative ways set up a city within a city, not a ghetto really, but a set of attitudes and a set of practices that eventually influenced the whole. For instance, more than half of the public school teachers in New York are Jews and roughly 80 per cent of the social workers.

Another reason why New York is "the Jewish city" is because of the reverse immigration. The ambitious young Jews of the Midwest and the South and the Northwest always came to New York City to make their mark in the arts, in law, or in business. And New York was the place where many Americans for the first time met Jews in any sizable numbers.

A Jewish peddler who ventured as far as Cincinnati in 1833 has described in a diary, preserved in the American Jewish Archives in that city, how he bent his head for the inspection of a Methodist minister's wife. She wanted to feel his horns. Not finding any, she told him in disappointment he was no different from others.

No doubt Middle America was better informed than this about biological properties at the turn of the century, but they still did not know about bagels and lox and potato pancakes and that the wife of an Orthodox Jew shaves her head on her marriage day lest her beauty ever distract her husband from his religious study.

Jews now work in probably every industry in the city, but that was not the case until after World War II. An advertising man once told me that not only were there no Jews in Madison Avenue agencies in the 1930s, but that Christian applicants who had not been graduated from Ivy League colleges were also discriminated against. Publishing, also a New York-based enterprise, had few Jews in its editorial offices, though what Jews there were made a lot of noise, like beleagured French Foreign Legionnaires singing to scare off the Riffs. The Jews in New York did not build the skyscrapers, nor did they burrow through the rivers to connect the tunnels.

But one Isidor Straus invented the department store when he bought out his partner, R. H. Macy; one David Dubinsky led a strike by the women blouse-makers which lasted twelve weeks, the longest strike in labor history up to that time; one superglove salesman named Samuel Goldfish decided he couldn't compete with importers making the most of the lowered tariff so he changed his name to Goldwyn and began making movies; and one poet named Emma Lazarus wrote a sonnet which was later placed on the pedestal of the Statue of Liberty.

That was enough. The Jews probably did not need rye bread to make the city a Jewish city.

And it is not premature to speak of the Golden Age of American Jewish culture, an age comparable to that which was experienced by our people in Spain from the eighth to the fifteenth centuries.

Jewish Americans number now more than three times the Jewish population of the State of Israel and twice that of Russia and all its satellites combined. What New York and America have given them is not only a refuge from persecution, but also a personal freedom and self-respect perhaps unsurpassed in the tri-millennial history of the Jews. That is already a matter of record. And it deserves to be remembered and recalled.

Jews comprise 3.2 per cent of the American people.

But they are seven times as numerous in New York as in the country as a whole. In the city one man in every four is a Jew. They are overwhelmingly English-speaking and native-born; economically, middle- and upper-middle class with a large proportion college-educated.

Today 1,836,000 live in the five boroughs of Greater New York —Manhattan, Brooklyn, the Bronx, Queens, and Richmond. Many more live in the adjacent suburban counties of Nassau, Suffolk, and Westchester. Altogether there are more Jews in the New York metropolitan area than in the State of Israel; one and a half times the number of Jews in all of Great Britain and Continental Europe outside the Soviet Union; and 40 per cent of the estimated 5,870,000 in the United States.

Of the five boroughs, Brooklyn today contains the largest Jewish population—760,000. Queens, which was once almost entirely German and Irish, is slowly but surely catching up. Its Jewish population is 420,000. This population growth reveals the mobility of the entire American middle class now moving from the city to the suburbs. The Borough of Queens is the gateway to Long Island, which stretches for a hundred miles into the Atlantic and has been one of the main suburban areas being populated by city residents moving out.

Within a brief span of twenty-five years vast communities of Jews have settled in the Long Island suburbs. Of course, as the Jews move in, the Gentiles retreat eastward on the island. And this is the pattern in all the other suburban areas. Another example: where once the Methodists congregated in the seacoast resorts of Asbury Park and Long Branch in central New Jersey, today these spas are almost wholly Jewish, the gentiles having fled further south.

The Borough of Manhattan, which is what visitors mean when they speak of New York, is still the focal point of the Jewish community. The Jews who live in Brooklyn, Queens, the Bronx, and Richmond, as well as in the suburbs of Long Island, northern New Jersey, and Westchester and Rockland counties, come to Manhattan, an island created by the Hudson and East Rivers and the bay. They come daily to Manhattan to work, for it supports the city's major business establishments, its principal government and cultural centers. Manhattan is also the headquarters for every city-wide Jewish organization as well as of all the national Jewish agencies and institutions save three. This concentration enables the national organizations to exercise a greater influence on the city's Jewish communal life than do the local Jewish agencies except for the two independent agencies which appeal to, and work for, the entire Jewish population of New York, the Federation of Jewish Philanthropies and the United Jewish Appeal of Greater New York.

In New York City the public schools are officially closed on Rosh Hashanah and Yom Kippur because a majority of the teachers are Jewish. Of the police force, numbering some thirty thousand, approximately three thousand are members of the Shomrim, the association of Jewish policemen; about a thousand Jews belong to the Naer Tormid Society, a similar organization of Jewish firemen; and there are fifteen thousand Jewish employees in New York City's branches of the United States Post Office.

I think these statistics about teachers, policemen, and firemen are important when one hears the charge that the Jews have all the money.

To this very day the big money, the real wealth of New York and of America, is still under tight control of the Protestant elite —the Episcopalians, Presbyterians, Congregationalists, and Baptists; the last named, though traditionally the poor of the agricultural rural sections of the American South, in the north jump into the first division with the Rockefellers of Standard Oil and the Chase Manhattan Bank. The ordinary uninformed visitor to New York might think the Jews have all the money, because the ordinary visitor sees the big Jewish department stores and the hundreds of Jewish specialty shops. But he does not see the insurance companies, nor does he meet officers of the railroads, utilities, airlines, nor does he invade the directorates of the big banks and U. S. Steel, General Motors, DuPont, Ford, Chrysler, Allied Chemical, Morgan Guaranty Trust, Dow Chemical, International Business Machines, General Dynamics, Eastman Kodak, or any of the new space industries.

The old-family Protestant elite turned the politics of the city over to the Irish, the Jews, the Italians, the Germans, and now the Negroes. They also left some of the manufacturing, retailing, and real estate to the ethnic minorities. This dispensation lets the Protestant elite go home, free of the city's peril, to Westchester County, ever northwest; to Long Island, ever eastward; or to the North Jersey coast, ever southward; and even to homes as far away as Connecticut, the Berkshire Mountains in Massachusetts, and the Pocono Mountains in Pennsylvania. And they go home every evening, unperturbed by the city's constant chaos.

Once in a while the Protestant elite is indeed disturbed. Street noises inundate their offices; they look out of their stock exchange, insurance, motor, steel, oil, and banking windows, to realize it's Saint Patrick's Day, or another strike, or a black Harlem boycott of white (often Jewish) stores. Once in a while the big-money Protestants miss the 5:15 commuter train because of the disturbance and crowds in the streets. They have to stand at the bar in Grand Central Station and wait for the 6:10.

Protestant elitism exists even in the legal profession where so many thousands of Irishmen, Jews, and Italians have become famous and wealthy as trial lawyers. The "financial" bar, however, the fellows who effect the mergers, the big tax lawyers, and those who represent the motor corporations, railroads, insurance companies, steamship lines, oil companies, new aircraft and space industries, the lawyers who act as liaison to government buying offices, four out of every five of these are of British or Scottish ancestry, mainly of colonial heritage.

Occasionally one of the elite with a memory of the old Whig tradition enters the political and civic life of the city. New York recently elected and re-elected John V. Lindsay as mayor, the second old-family Protestant to hold that office since 1900.

In the main, the Irish, Italians, and Jews have run the city for nearly a century. The Negroes have achieved some political power since the late 1940s. As the sons and the grandsons of the old Irish sachems of the political organization known as Tammany Hall moved outward and upward into industry and the professions, the Italians took over many of the local political organizations. The Negroes are now edging in on the Italians. The Irish, Italians, and Negroes also control the civil service positions with tenure. They are the court clerks, bailiffs, jailers, policemen, and investigators. You will find the Jews among the teachers, social workers, and welfare administrators.

But when the outlander talks of New York as "a Jewish city," he is right, even if it is usually for the wrong reasons. It is a Jewish city because the attitudes, culture, art, theaters, stores, fashions, music, writing, television, and most of the producers and directors, artists, and architects are Jewish. The imagination and style of the city comes from Jewish *chutzpa*—for which read imagination and guts. More and more Yiddish dialect passes into common parlance and more and more of the Jewish diet becomes a city staple. When the Mets won the World Series, the New York *Daily News* carried the headline: METS WIN SERIES —MAZELTOV. Most New Yorkers know what *megillah* and *shlemiel* mean and most New Yorkers have eaten blintzes and what they call "Jewish rye bread."

I offer none of this of course in an apologetic spirit. The entry of New York's immigrant Jews into the American open society within a single generation is a remarkable achievement. There are now vast Jewish business establishments, many of great wealth, particularly in the garment industry. While over a half-million Jewish wage-earners are in private industry and in government, nearly 20 per cent of the Jews in New York are self-employed, in dozens of professions, and in business as agents, brokers, dealers, and salesmen. Still, despite the great Jewish business enterprises, the half-million Jewish wage earners make New York nearly the only city in the United States with a Jewish proletariat.

History was on the side of the Jews' adaptability to the New World and specifically to the conditions of New York City. The early Church fathers had relegated them to the ghetto as a punishment and as a form of "protection" for the Gentiles. But the primitive Church had no suspicion that it was giving the Jews a one-thousand-year head start in living in the industrial complex of the twentieth century. The Jew was an urban man before there were words for "city slicker" and "country hick."

A point worth repeating is that the great wealth of America is still securely in the hands of the ethnic elite—the Protestants.

This is the conclusion reached after an intensive survey conducted by *Fortune* magazine some ten years ago and more recently by such social analysts as William Miller (*Man in Business*, Harper & Row, 1962) and Moses Rischin (*The American Gospel of Success*, Quadrangle, 1966).

A grocer in Iowa goes out of business, a contractor in north Florida goes broke, a café owner in Arkansas has to shut down for lack of customers, and the lament is the same: *The Jews in New York have made things tough all over, they control the money. Who can compete against them?* Of course this is a myth, a convenient excuse to avoid facing one's own failures and an assumption that contradicts the facts of economic reality. But it is important to clarify and correct this stereotype of Jews-and-money as inseparable for another reason as well: because the relationship of Jews-and-art is still one of the best-kept secrets of New York, of America, and of the world.

From the early decades of this century down to the present time, Jewish authors, painters, playwrights, musicians, actors, and entrepreneurs in the various arts have played leading roles in the cultural life of New York City, which is to say, the Western Hemisphere. In 1906 the celebrated British actress Ellen Terry arrived in New York to commence an American tour and insisted on appearing at the Neighborhood Playhouse to give the immigrant Jews a performance of her famous *Readings from Shakespeare*. It was a gala night in the ghetto.

In 1913 a French author named Pierre Loti visited New York and wrote a highly critical article about his sojourn in the city. All the New York papers answered with angry comment, but the editors overlooked the one kind thing Loti had to say: "The Israelites here support the arts, the only bearable comfort in this city."

## The Yiddish Theater

The Jews in New York got their early training in theatergoing with the Yiddish theater, which came into prominence as early as the 1880s. Next to the press, the stage has been the most potent cultural influence in the life of the Jewish immigrants.

Theatergoing was traditional among the immigrant Jews. One

social critic remarked, "Nine out of every ten Jews goes to the theater, while one out of every ten Jews goes to synagogue."

So much a habit was it that in the early days three theaters were deriving large profits from catering to Jewish audiences alone. All three of these theaters, with seating capacities equal to the largest patronized by the non-Jewish elements of the city's population (one built for the specific purpose of housing a Yiddish stock company), were located within five minutes' walk of each other in the downtown ghetto. Another, in the newer but rapidly growing and more prosperous Harlem ghetto, failed. There were five Yiddish theaters up to a recent date and there may be that number again shortly. It is estimated that the patrons of the Yiddish theaters numbered from five thousand to seven thousand a night, and as performances were given on each of the seven nights in the week, with two matinees (Saturday and Sunday), the importance of the theater as a source of amusement in the ghetto may be imagined.

The Yiddish theater was a cross between a soap opera and university studies. It presented to its audience the conflicts engendered in the process of becoming an American. It stated the attitudes and counterattitudes of an immigrant milieu on a week-to-week basis. Few plays lasted longer than four nights. Their literary quality was, to say the least, suspect.

The themes always dealt with the conflict between the older, immigrant generation and the younger, assimilating generation. In addition, the Yiddish theater often had weddings staged after the show. And amateur night was initiated at Miner's Theater.

The Yiddish theater was socialistic in character and owed its profits to the motives of charity. Every performance was a "benefit." On the Lower East Side you rarely heard the statement, "I'm going to the theater," but rather, "I'm going to a benefit." Along with the prohibition "Post No Bills" and the important phrase "working papers," "benefit" was one of the first English words the Jewish immigrant learned.

At one time or another, lodges and societies of the Lower East Side (of which there were a countless number) bought a theater "benefit"; that is, they paid the management a certain sum of money for a performance, a little over half of the box-office receipts assuming every seat were occupied. A committee of the organization selected a play to be presented on the night of the benefit. The tickets were sold by the members of the society and every dollar received over the price paid to the management was the society's profit. This was no philanthropy on the part of the theater managers; on the contrary, it was good business. The theaters were reasonably certain of crowded houses on Friday, Saturday, and Sunday evenings and at the matinees on Saturday and Sunday afternoons, but the other nights of the week were not lucrative. Without these benefits the theaters would no doubt have run into financial difficulties.

It was on benefit nights that the Yiddish theater was at its vivid best. The audience was made up of family parties and neighborhood groups—from the grandfather to the infant, and including the boarder: the whole tenement house was there in bedlam with box lunches. Half the audience had never been to the theater before and would probably never have come at all, but they could not "insult" by not buying tickets. Furthermore, it was a *mitzvah* (good deed) to contribute to the cause for which the benefit was given. And having earned the mitzvah, why not partake of the earthly joy in its train?

My father, Reb Lebche, was president of the Mikulinczer Verein (Galicia) and he was in charge of hundreds of benefits for his society. Twice a year the Mikulinczer benefit was to provide dowries for unmarried girls in the Jewish community of Mikulincz in what was then Austro-Hungarian Empire.

A Mikulinczer benefit operated much the way a milk fund benefit operates today. The organization bought every seat in the house at a discount, sold the tickets to members and friends at more than list price, and the net profit went to the designated cause.

My father always made a speech between the second and third acts of the benefits he sponsored. He owned a cutaway coat and a huge silk hat and was so articulate he made the women weep when he spoke. And as the Mikulinczer Verein gave a benefit to help unmarried girls, so did the anarchists give up talking treason to hold a benefit for fellow members imprisoned in Siberia.

The cost of a benefit ticket ranged between twenty-five cents and one dollar. On Friday, Saturday, and Sunday performances, however, the house could always sell out at $1.25—this despite the fact that two of these performances would fall on the Sabbath, Friday night and the Saturday matinee, a time when an Orthodox Jew will undertake no activity save walking to the *shul*.

# Thalia Theatre טעאטער־ארבית

| | | |
|---|---|---|
| G. AMBERG, | - - - - - - - | Lessee |
| S. MOGULESKO and M. HEINE | - - - - - | Managers |
| M. HOROWITZ, | - - Author \| I. EDELSTEIN, - | Secretary |

## Thursday Evening, February 12.

# Rachel and Leah

### Periodical Sketch in 4 Acts and 12 Scenes, by Jacobson.

#### Music by Mr. Mogulesko.

##### CAST OF CHARACTERS.

| | |
|---|---|
| Herman Rosencranz, a workingman........................ | Mr. Kessler |
| Rachel, his wife ..................................... | Mrs. Deine |
| Leah, her sister....................................... | Mrs. Deine |
| Robert, their child................................... | Miss Weissman |
| Solomon Feinstein, a banker, father of Rachel and Leah....... | Mr. Neiman |
| Nathan Grossman, his nephew......................... | Mr. Gold |
| Fuksman, his partner, an usurer ....................... | Mr. Greenberg |
| Leon, Herman's cousin, a workingman................... | Mr. Heine |
| Blume, his wife....................................... | Miss Rosin |
| Abraham.... } Herman's friends ) ..................... | Mr. Wachtel |
| Goldman.... } { ..................... | Mr. Marienstrass |
| Schwartz, a drunkard.................................. | Mr. Wachtel |
| Dinah, Schwartz's love................................ | Miss Sidelsky |
| Rosman, Blume's father................................ | Mr. Semenoff |
| Joseph his son....................................... | Mr. Wachtel |
| A detective.......................................... | Mr. Marienstras |

##### Peasants, Guests, etc.

| | |
|---|---|
| Musical Director ................................ | Prof. Hellman |
| Master Machinist................................ | Chas. B. Hauschild |

The three most famous Yiddish theaters were the People's Theater, the Windsor, and the Thalia. The Thalia was the ritziest; you couldn't take a baby inside.

But the American ethic is a persuasive ethic, and the theaters, for better or for worse, were crowded with the Orthodox on the Sabbath. There were many whose consciences still gnawed at them which they eased by heckling an actor whose role desecrated the Sabbath. The audience would yell, "Smoking a cigar on the Sabbath, boo boo boo!" The actor would look startled at the hypocrites who should have been in shul themselves at that very moment.

At the height of Jewish immigration from Europe there were fourteen theaters in New York producing drama, musicals, and

Jacob Gordin was the premier Yiddish playwright. He wrote about fifty plays and Jacob P. Adler was the actor in them. Among his best plays were *Siberia, The Jewish King Lear, The Slaughter,* and *The Wild One.* He brought realism to the Yiddish stage. Often his plays adapted patterns of ghetto life with surprising fidelity.

Gordin was connected with Adler for many years. Gordin's dramas were the only plays on contemporary life which Adler thought worthy of presentation.

Mayor William J. Gaynor dedicated the David Kessler Theater on Second Avenue in 1911. The name of the play was Jacob Gordin's *Gott, Mensch, und Teufel (God, Man, and Devil)*.

adaptations in Yiddish. Geographically, the Yiddish theater was located in several community centers, verein auditoriums, and lecture halls. Of the legitimate theaters, five were prominent—the People's Theater, the Windsor, Miner's, the Thalia, and David Kessler's Second Avenue Theater. The Thalia was the ritziest; it allowed no babies.

But if the Thalia wasn't filled with mewling infants, it was certainly filled with shouting vendors. When the first-act curtain rang down, the aisles were filled with boys and men hawking ice cream, charlotte russes, and anarchist pamphlets. And sometimes they didn't wait for the curtain but surreptitiously started down the aisles while actors delivered their lines. Most of the immigrants who attended were young boys and girls whose parents had sent them on to America. And they wept, remembering their families in the old country. On Saturday afternoons, the Thalia Theater was filled with shop girls who had a good cry listening to Lucy Gherman sing "The *Eibega* Mama" (The Eternal Mother).

The Yiddish audience was composed of the factory worker, peddler, shopkeeper, anarchist, socialist, rabbi, scholar, and journalist. And the institution of the theater served yet another function which has never been adequately explored. The *shadchen* (professional matchmaker) used the Yiddish theater as the most convenient (and elevating) place for his couples to hold their first meeting. After preliminary discussion with each of the families, he gave one ticket to the girl and the other to the boy. It gave the couple a chance to see each other without embarrassment or overcommitment. At the end of the evening they could say, one to the other, "I hope to see you again," without any definite invitation, and that was that, or the girl could invite the fellow to her home, which gave him still another chance to get out of it. But if he accepted, it indicated that a deal was on the way.

So the performance itself was only the beginning of the "Yiddish theater." It was a culture that involved around-the-clock arguments in the coffee houses, occupied pages of newsprint, and often divided families in fierce discussions over the relative merits of "the show" or the playwrights. Everybody was a critic, and the morning after a performance the fellow pressing pants in the factory would give his "review" of the opening the night before. Invariably he would say it was a *shmatte* (a rag—a nothing). To some pants-pressers everything was a shmatte—Ibsen, Shaw, or Sudermann not excepted. The intellectuals did not spare the playwrights, and Jacob Gordin, the most prolific playwright, was also the most controversial figure in the Yiddish theater. Some others, among them Solomon Libin and Leon Kobrin, managed to get attention, and not without success; they were disciples of Gordin who at times ventured farther than their master. But Gordin had literary skill and powers. If he had been tolerant of criticism and amenable to discipline, he would have become the greatest personal influence on the development of the Yiddish stage. Although he wrote many plays which he probably regarded as greater, his *Jewish King Lear* was his most popular. The general consensus is that *God, Man, and Devil* was his greatest and unquestionably a lasting contribution to the literature of the drama.

After a Gordin opening, the theatergoers waited for the inevitable blast from the editor of the *Jewish Daily Forward*, Mr. Abe Cahan. His invective and satire often made a better "play" than Gordin had written. From there the coffee houses would take up the matter, and many a rolled-up newspaper came down on the head of a strong Gordin (or Cahan) supporter.

But the actors were above criticism. Their popularity and presence inspired myths. It was said of Jacob Latteiner, who wrote and acted in over a hundred plays, that he improvised one in the afternoon by dressing himself in the costumes of the different characters and walking on in each role while the other actors feverishly took notes. I knew many Jews who swore to this, but I knew just as many who swore they were at the ball park the day Babe Ruth called his homer. Actors used to say of Professor Moses Hurwitz that they did not have to memorize their sides in any new play because the dialogue was substantially the same as his last. All his heroes and villains were alike.

People had their favorite actors, and where the big three were involved—Jacob Adler, David Kessler, and Boris Thomashefsky—there was considerable argument, but all were highly respected. In fact, until their children discovered ballplayers like Ty Cobb and Christy Mathewson, the immigrants virtually made folk heroes out of the actors.

Thomashefsky was a matinee idol, particularly after he appeared in tights in one of his musicals. He had gigantic thighs, which caused many a sigh among the immigrant women at a time when heft was still a mark of beauty. Adler was a source of great pride to the community because of the recognition he had

Jacob P. Adler, the folk hero of the ghetto.

earned as an artist beyond the borders of the Yiddish world. When my father said "Yakob Adler," it sounded like a whispered prayer.

To the Jews of the Lower East Side, Jacob Adler was to other Yiddish actors what Zeus was to the other gods on Olympus. The curtains were always decorated with advertisements, and when Adler returned to the theater after an illness, he had a big red ad hung at the People's Theater which read, THE SPLENDID EAGLE SPREADS HIS WINGS AGAIN.

He was a living legend. He always traveled with a coterie of hangers-on, and when he settled himself at an East Side coffeehouse, he always had a couple of flunkies warding off the worshipers as he washed down caviar and eggs and potato *varenikis* with huge goblets of Rhine wine and seltzer. One of the flunkies sat so close to Adler that he became known as "K'mat Adler," which meant "Almost Adler."

Once when Adler was on tour, before a particular performance, a handsome young woman with a two-year-old child got through to the great man's dressing room. Adler turned from the mirror and the woman began her story. "Mr. Adler, you remember me? When you were here three years ago, you invited me to supper after the performance, you remember?" With this she pushed a little boy ahead of her, "And this is the result, this little boy is your own son."

Adler looked at the child with satisfaction and said, "That's a nice boy, a real nice boy." He reached into his dresser drawer and gave her two tickets. "Take them, you'll like the show." The woman was disappointed, and she stammered, "But Mr. Adler, this is your son; we don't need tickets, we need bread."

Adler was hurt; he flung the tickets back into the drawer. "Bread you need! If you want bread you screw a baker. I am an actor. From me you get tickets."

Yet many of the experts believed that David Kessler was the greatest actor of them all. When he opened his Second Avenue Theater with *God, Man, and Devil*, important theatrical figures of Broadway attended. It was Kessler who coached Enrico Caruso when the great Italian tenor was preparing his role as Eleazar in *La Juive*.

Of the women of the Yiddish stage, it need only be said that Bertha Kalich was an actress of such rare ability that critics said

Jacob Adler as Shylock. *Shylock* and *The Jewish King Lear* were the two most memorable adaptations for the Yiddish stage.

she was as good as Sarah Bernhardt at Sarah's best, but never as bad as Sarah at Sarah's worst.

By far the favorite playwright of the Lower East Side was William Shakespeare. I believe that eventually all of his plays were translated into Yiddish and adapted for the Jewish stage. Of course, these dramas were appreciably different from what they were when the Elizabethans first saw them at the Globe Theater.

The Yiddish *Hamlet* (*Yeshiva Bucher*) opened not on the castle wall but with the wedding feast. Claudius was no king, however, but a rabbi who occupied a position of prestige in a Russian village. Though Claudius was not portrayed as a murderer, he had metaphorically killed the king by wooing and winning Queen Gertrude. Young Hamlet arrives, fresh from his ordination as a rabbi and turns the wedding feast into a funeral. The party degenerates into scenes of quarrels between Gertrude and Hamlet, Ophelia and Hamlet, Polonius (a merchant) and Hamlet. The wicked Claudius conspires against Hamlet, convincing the villagers that he is a nihilist who does not believe in God. But Hamlet uncovers the plot, and the uncle is exiled to Siberia.

The most popular of all the adapted Shakespearean plays was *The Jewish King Lear. King Lear* was a natural—a play about bad daughters and good daughters and the misery of an aged father. In the Yiddish *King Lear*, Goneril and Regan leave their father's house to marry Gentiles, while Cordelia stays faithfully by his side.

The popularity of the Yiddish theater began to decline in the 1930s, when the children of the immigrants left the Lower East Side for the open areas of Riverside Drive, the Bronx, and Westchester and Fairfield counties. A theater is only as popular as its language. As spoken Yiddish perceptively diminished, so did the theater decline.

But at its peak, it was one of the most productive of all theaters —and one of the most glamorous.

The performers who made the jump from the Yiddish to the American stage would make a respectable Who's Who of the American theater: Paul Muni, Edward G. Robinson, Luther and Stella Adler, Jacob Ben-Ami, Menasha Skulnik, Mollie Picon, Maurice Schwartz, Joseph Schildkraut, Gertrude Berg and many others, including my friends the Bernardis—Boris Bernardi, man-

ager of the touring company of *Once Upon a Mattress*, and
Herschel Bernardi, who played Lieutenant Jacoby on the *Peter
Gunn* television series, Tevye in *Fiddler on the Roof*, and also
Harry Golden in the West Coast production of *Only in America*,
by Jerry Lawrence and Bob Lee.

Yiddish theater was a world filled to overflowing with humor.
There must be many of my contemporaries who remember the
famous Grossman poster announcing a new *pyessa* (piece—a new
show): "Samuel B. Grossman, Producer and Actor, presents *The
Sorrowing Father*, a new play in Three Acts by Samuel B. Gross-
man; with Irving Grossman, Joseph Grossman, Helen Grossman;
Music by B. S. Grossman. For benefits write to Treasurer Joseph
Grossman."

But the Jewish audiences in New York will not support a bad
play or musical, as recently, for example, they refused to support
Leon Uris' *Ari*.

Bertha Kalich. Bertha Kalich first appeared
on the Yiddish speaking stage in such
productions as *The Delayed Wedding, East
Side Ghetto, A Doll's House*, and *Magda*.
Her English-speaking debut was made in
1905 in *Fédora*. Her greatest success was in
*The Kreutzer Sonata*. In 1932 a testimonial
performance was given in her honor at the
Yiddish Art Theater to celebrate the fortieth
anniversary of her first appearance on the
stage. A second testimonial was given in her
honor by her English-speaking colleagues at
the Vanderbilt Theater.

New York City is the greatest Jewish city in the world because the source of its creativity is mostly Jewish. It is the greatest accomplishment of the Jewish people since the Jerusalem of King Solomon. At the same time and closely related to their outstanding performance in the arts, the Jews of New York have achieved pre-eminence in philanthropy and in scholarship and other intellectual activities. As for the arts, look at the list of prominent New York Jews that follows.

When Jan Peerce, the Metropolitan Opera star, was in the Soviet Union, the number requested by his Jewish audience most often was the simple folk song, "Rozhinkes mit Mandlen" (Raisins and Almonds). Those elderly Jews in the Soviet, cut off from Jewish communal living, folkways, and culture, wanted this great American tenor to sing a folk song to bring them a bit of their past: mother, father, home, and memory.

Mr. Peerce's experience was identical to one related by Irving Berlin. It happened the day after the Americans entered Rome in 1944. Berlin and his troupe of GI actors arranged a show to which hundreds of Italian civilians were invited. This was the first free theatrical performance these Italians had seen in twenty years. Under Mussolini, as well as under Hitler, their culture had been "regulated," and no matter how hard Irving and his troupe tried, they received very little response from the Italians, and they could not understand it. Finally, Irving thought of the Lower East Side where he was raised, near Little Italy, and he had an inspiration. He went to the center of the stage and in his high-pitched voice sang that old Italian song, "Oi Marie, Oi Marie. . . ." The Italians rose in their seats; first they cheered, then they wept for joy. Here in Rome, the capital of the entire operatic world, the Italians poured their hearts out to a simple little folk song, "Oi Marie," just as the elderly Jews of the Soviet wanted "Rozhinkes mit Mandlen" to bring them so much closer to home.

I once walked over to Pell Street, in the heart of Chinatown, and stood in front of number 20. The glass in the window was black with the dust and grime of years, but, after a few minutes, the door opened and I was able to peek inside. There was a group of ragged old men, including a Chinese, picking over some rags and paper. It looked like a salvage business.

This was where Irving Berlin wrote his first song. It was a saloon in those days, known as "Nigger Mike's." Nigger Mike was not a Negro, but a Romanian Jew, who was given the name because of his dark complexion. His real name was Mike Salter. Irving Berlin, as Izzy Baline, got his first job there as a singing waiter. It was while working for Nigger Mike that he wrote his first song, "Marie from Sunny Italy."

A few years later, Berlin got a job with the famous prize fighter Jimmy Jelly, who owned a café of his own. Soon thereafter the entire world was humming "Alexander's Ragtime Band," and Irving Berlin was on his way.

Millions of American boys have marched off to three wars singing Berlin's tunes: "Oh! How I Hate to Get Up in the Morning," "A Pretty Girl Is Like a Melody," "God Bless America," "Remember," "White Christmas," "There's No Business Like Show Business," and hundreds of others. From a singing waiter in a Bowery joint to the position where he earned fifteen million dollars for Army relief with his show, *This Is the Army*—all within the lifetime of an immigrant boy. You can say it again, "God Bless America."

Unequivocally called "the greatest tenor in the world" by *Time* magazine and "the Met's second Caruso" by *The Saturday Evening Post*, Richard Tucker found himself recently the focus of a nation-wide "Silver Jubilee" celebration, as the Metropolitan Opera Association and the legions of Tucker fans everywhere joined to honor the twenty-fifth anniversary (in January 1970) of his now historic Metropolitan debut. It commemorated a quarter of a century during which tenors have come and gone, but during which Richard Tucker has astonishingly continued to heap success upon dazzling success, setting the standard and providing the inspiration for an entire generation of singers.

Still an ordained cantor, entitled to perform weddings and funerals, Tucker foregoes all opera and concert engagements twice a year to return to the ministry for the fall Jewish High Holy Days and the traditional spring Passover Seder services. In the summer of 1963, while on a concert tour of Israel, he agreed to officiate at Sabbath morning services at the Great Synagogue in Tel Aviv. Overflow crowds jammed the aisles and firemen wearing prayer shawls over their uniforms were called in to maintain order. At the end of the ritual, hundreds formed a procession behind Tucker through the downtown streets of the Israeli metropolis as he led them singing Sabbath hymns.

Leonard Bernstein conducted the Philharmonic Symphony and is a composer and a pianist. His works include "Clarinet Sonata," "Jeremiah Symphony," and the musicals *On the Town* and *West Side Story*. He was the recipient of the Television Academy award in 1960 for his young people's concerts.

Admittedly one of the great coloraturas of our time, as well as one of America most beloved and respected artists, Roberta Peters is heard in the Metropolitan Opera House in several of her most highly acclaimed roles. Since her spectacular, unheralded debut in 1950 at the Metropolitan, as Zerlina in *Don Giovanni*, when she was suddenly called upon to substitute for an ailing artist, the glamorous soprano has consistently added to the laurels bestowed upon her then by critics. Proclaimed a diva at nineteen, she has demonstrated her permanent right to that title in succeeding years.

George Gershwin captured and expressed in his music the color and rhythm of the American scene, the scent and even the characteristic mental slant of the American people. An example of this quality is found in the opening themes of "An American in Paris." Equally typical in its Americanism is his campaign song from *Of Thee I Sing*, "Wintergreen for President." In 1923 he composed his famous "Rhapsody in Blue" and until his death fourteen years later Gershwin advanced steadily in musicianship, an accruing and mastery of form, a consummate skill in symphonic orchestration, and a more sustained power of expression, until finally *Porgy and Bess* revealed every facet of Gershwin's genius.

Ira Gershwin. One of America's great lyricists, he wrote words for much of his brother George's music as well as for other composers including Kurt Weill, Vincent Youmans, and Jerome Kern.

The sons of Jewish immigrants from Eastern Europe, as a matter of fact, did more to romanticize the South than Margaret Mitchell's *Gone With the Wind*. George Gershwin and Irving Caesar wrote "Swanee," Irving Berlin "When the Midnight Choo Choo Leaves for Alabam'," Benny Davis "Carolina Moon," Jack Yellen "How's Ev'ry Little Thing in Dixie?" and "Alabama Jubilee," and Gus Kahn "Carolina in the Morning."

Irving Caesar is one of America's all-time great song writers. He has collaborated on songs with some of the most talented writers of the twentieth century, including George Gershwin, Vincent Youmans, Victor Herbert, Sigmund Romberg, Rudolf Friml, and Ray Henderson. His list is headed with such everyday titles as "Tea for Two," "Sometimes I'm Happy," "I Want to Be Happy," "Crazy Rhythm," "Swanee," "Just a Gigolo" and "Is It True What They Say About Dixie?"

I suspect the drive of immigrant boys was to become an American as quickly as possible and they identified the South with the most American section of the country. You can see how Irving Caesar from P.S. 20 on Rivington Street tore his heart out in George Gershwin's "Swanee."

And Oscar Hammerstein and Jerome Kern with their "Ol' Man River" and Phil Harris forever singing "That's What I Like About the South."

Morris Rosenfeld wrote his poetry in Yiddish but the translations into English caused him to be adopted by the Gentiles in the labor movement who wanted Rosenfeld for their own. "He is a class poet," they said, "a worker's poet." These friendly critics cited for an example Rosenfeld's *All for Naught:*

> Smash your pen, wretched poet!
> Who needs your song, your lyric art,
> In this discordant, frantic land
> Which clamors like a noisy mart,
> Where frenzied people rush about,
> Where every sound's a hue and cry,
> Where every man lives by his wits
> And barely has the time to die.

Lionel Trilling is a writer and university professor and one of the most eminent critics in America. He is the author of *Matthew Arnold, E. M. Forster, The Middle of the Journey, The Liberal Imagination, Freud and the Crisis of Our Culture, A Gathering of Fugitives, Beyond Culture: Essays on Learning and Literature, Experiences of Literature,* and *Essays On the Life and Literature of Sigmund Freud.* He is professor of English at Columbia University.

Norman Podhoretz, editor of the American Jewish Committee-sponsored periodical *Commentary*, is a graduate of Cambridge University in England with first class honors in English. He has written dozens of articles and reviews for the leading magazines in America, and is the author of *Doings and Undoings: The Fifties and After in American Writing* and of *Making It*. He is a member of the Seminar on American Civilization at Columbia University.

The American Jewish Congress. In 1933 I went to a meeting of the American Jewish Congress and I heard Rabbi Stephen S. Wise tell the audience that the new chancellor of Germany, Adolf Hitler, not only meant to persecute the Jews but to kill them, exterminate them. He told of his visit to Germany where he warned the Jews of their coming persecution. But they laughed at him, "You've got the Ku Klux Klan in America," they said, "and we have Adolf Hitler here." The same night that he spoke, Rabbi Wise organized the first worldwide countermovement against Nazi persecution, an intensive boycott of German goods and services. During this entire period the American Jewish Congress was greatly concerned in protecting American Jews against defamation and discrimination.

In 1945 it established its Commission on Law and Social Action, setting as its goal the attainment of "full equality in a free society for all Americans." The commission has had three main areas of concern: freedom of religion, including vigorous enforcement of the constitutional guarantee of separation of church and state; freedom of expression, including protection of the right to protest; and, of course, civil rights. In that area, the American Jewish Congress (AJC) has treated the fight against all forms of discrimination based on race, religion, and national origin as a "seamless web." It believes that no minority is secure as long as any other minority is persecuted. Conversely, it believes that a victory over discrimination against any one minority benefits all others.

Rabbi Arthur J. Lelyveld is the president and Joseph Robison director of Commission on Law and Social Action. Will Maslow, the executive director of the American Jewish Congress has written many valuable books on civil rights and law.

Irving M. Engel, president of the American Jewish Committee from 1954 to 1959, led this great Jewish organization into the civil rights movement on behalf of the Negroes. He is the honorary director of the Educational Foundation for Jewish Girls, which is now in its ninetieth year. The doors of the foundation are open on a non-sectarian basis to the girls and women whose educational goals and financial need merit its support. In general, it requires a legal residence within a sixty-mile radius of Manhattan. Each applicant is considered on an individual basis. There is no geographic limitation as to the location of the accredited institution that is essential for the achievement of the applicant's goals.

Scholarships in the form of grants and loans are awarded for one year and are renewable subject to each applicant's record and continuing financial need. Over the years an ever-growing number of referring schools, colleges, universities, and agencies of all kinds have been the chief source of applicants for the foundation's aid.

About one fourth of its four hundred current scholarship recipients are in graduate school, studying medicine, social work, law, dentistry, and a variety of academic disciplines—receiving annual awards as large as $2500 in loans and grants. About 250 undergraduates are studying in some seventy different colleges here and abroad. The remainder of the scholarship recipients study in community colleges, vocational schools, evening programs, and summer schools. Applicants come from all walks of life. For the most part, they have already made considerable personal sacrifice in their efforts to continue their chosen courses of study.

Emma Lazarus (1849–87) was a poet and essayist. Her early work attracted the attention of William Cullen Bryant and Ralph Waldo Emerson. It remained for an emotional rather than a cultural shock to stir Emma Lazarus to an awareness of Jewish life. She visited Ellis Island where she saw hundreds of poor Jews awaiting admission to the United States. Poignantly she realized she, too, was a Jew. She learned Hebrew and undertook the English translation of the German ballads of Heine. She organized meetings of Jewish leaders out of which eventually developed the Hebrew Technical Institute of New York.

When the French gave the Statue of Liberty to the people of the United States, Emma Lazarus wrote a sonnet which was sold at auction along with original manuscripts by Walt Whitman, Mark Twain, and Bret Harte, as her contribution to the fund raised to provide a pedestal for the colossal figure of "Liberty Enlightening the World." The Statue of Liberty was mounted above this pedestal on Bedloe's Island in New York Harbor in 1884. Emma Lazarus died in 1887, but in 1903 the lines of her sonnet, *The New Colossus*, were inscribed on a bronze tablet inside the pedestal. The last five lines are the most memorable:

> ". . . Give me your tired, your poor,
> Your huddled masses yearning to breathe free,
> The wretched refuse of your teeming shore.
> Send these, the homeless, tempest-tost to me:
> I lift my lamp beside the golden door."

Walter Lippmann is an outstanding writer on public affairs, government, the organization of society, and the political and cultural trends of the world at a time when these subjects engage the world as never before. When Lippmann came to his respected position in American life in the early 1930s he was a little over forty years old. His background was wide and varied, exactly what the times called for. He wrote a book, *A Preface to Politics*, which described the searching out of impulses and motives which underlie human action in the political field. He was a friend of Theodore Roosevelt and Woodrow Wilson while he was editor of the New York *World*. And the late President John F. Kennedy went from his inauguration to the home of Walter Lippmann to visit with him a while.

Besides *A Preface to Politics*, his books include *The Political Scene, Liberty and the News, Men of Destiny, A Preface to Morals, The United States in World Affairs*, and *Some Notes on War and Peace*.

August Belmont, the American Rothschild, raised and equipped the first German-born regiment sent from New York City during the Civil War. It was August Belmont who not only secured European loans for Abraham Lincoln but actually stopped a movement in England to recognize the Confederacy.

The Dictionary of American Biography estimates that Belmont's most valuable service, perhaps, was a constant correspondence with financial and political leaders in Europe, including the Rothschilds, in which he set forth forcibly the Union side of the great conflict.

In 1849 August Belmont married Caroline Perry, daughter of Commodore Matthew Perry who was later to open up Japan for trade beginning with an official visit in 1852. Miss Perry was an

Episcopalian and when President Franklin Pierce appointed August Belmont as minister to the Netherlands, nativist Whigs at-
tacked the selection because, they said, Belmont was a Jew. To
one such attack the *Asmonean*, a Jewish literary journal, could
find no better response than to deny that Belmont was a Jew because he had married an Episcopalian.

Ernestine Rose (born in Piotrkow, Russian Poland in 1810; her
maiden name was Potowski), was the wife of William Rose and
the daughter of a rabbi. As early as 1852, she spearheaded the
American movement for women's liberation.

As "a child of Israel," Mrs. Rose pleaded for equal rights of her
sex. She said:

"Woman is a slave, from the cradle to the grave. Father,
guardian, husband—master still. One conveys her, like a piece of
property, over to the other. She is said to have been created only
for man's benefit, not for her own. This falsehood is the main
cause of her inferior education and position. Man has arrogated
to himself the right to her person, her property, and her children;
and so vitiated is public opinion, that if a husband is rational and
just enough to acknowledge the influence of his wife, he is called
'henpecked.' The term is not very elegant, but it is not of my
coining, and I suppose we all know what it means. But it is high
time these irrationalities are done away, for the whole race suffers
by it. In claiming our rights, we claim the rights of humanity;
it is not for the interest of woman only, but for the interest of all.
The interests of the sexes cannot be separated—together they
must enjoy or suffer—both are one in the race."

Mrs. Rose was chairman of a women's rights convention at
Syracuse, New York, in 1861 in which she advocated the franchise
for women. She stated that since women must pay the same rent
and taxes as men, they should enjoy the same rights.

" 'Tis not well that man be alone—mother, sister, wife, daughter
or woman must be with him to keep him in his proper sphere.
Look about you and you will perceive the rude, uncultivated air
of Adam before Eve civilized him by making him partake of the
Tree of Knowledge."

Mrs. Rose insisted that the word "obey" should be taken out
of the marriage ritual. She would substitute the far better word
"assist." As a companion to man, she would be more of an in-
structor and as a member of society, more useful and happy.

The above obviously provides only a few examples of outstanding American Jews. "In proportion to population," writes Nathaniel Weyl, *The Creative Elite in America* (Public Affairs Press, Washington, D.C.), "the outstanding element in the intellectual leadership of the United States is the Jew . . . The reasons for Jewish pre-eminence are multiple, complex, and subject to many qualifications as to their reach in space and time . . . At this stage it is sufficient to suggest that the fundamental reason for the observed differences is that Jewry bred selectively for intelligence during centuries in which Christendom bred selectively against it."

It is also true, Weyl points out, that the Jews of Europe, though outside society, were better off since their isolation protected them. The War of the Roses decimated English peerage; the Crusades decimated the nobility and soldiery of Europe. The Jews had a biogenetic advantage; the best of their young people were insulated from the bloody internecine wars of the Continent. They honed this advantage with study and school.

I am willing to bet that between 1905 and 1914 there were more classrooms in operation in the fifteen square blocks of the Lower East Side than in some of the states of the Union. There were night schools, day schools, before-going-to-work schools, private schools, business schools, schools for learning English, and classes in "civics" (protocol for learning to be a citizen). There were schools located in tenement houses conducted by fellows who had come to America only a year before, and schools in settlement houses conducted by eighth-generation Christian social workers.

The classes and lectures at union halls inspired a loyalty and fellowship, and the excitement of learning always electrified them. Union halls are not often electrically charged today—except when there's a strike vote and the members sing "Solidarity Forever."

When some of the ghetto walls of Europe began coming down, first because of the Napoleonic Wars, then because of revolutionary fervor of the 1840s, Jews still found themselves in a hostile society. They feared that emancipation was a delusion. They discovered that Jewishness was a barrier and a disability in a wide range of social relations and that citizenship opened far fewer doors than imagined.

Then, by the middle of the nineteenth century, they made a wild dash to the universities of Europe. They had been inspired by the great Jewish poet Heinrich Heine who had warned, "Remember we must be twice as good to get half as much." They were undertaking early an apprenticeship that would equip them superbly for life in the industrial society of the twentieth century. Education was to become the key for entry into the middle class of America. Seventy per cent of the New York Jews completed high school as against 49 per cent of the rest of the population. Nineteen per cent are college graduates as against 8.6 per cent of the rest of the population. Almost no Jews fail to get further than elementary school, but nearly one fifth of all the other whites had less than eight years of school. And whereas seven out of ten Jews in the age group twenty-one to forty-five attended a minimum of a year at college, the total for the entire white population was only one out of four.

Education was the key to everything. You walked up to your flat in a tenement house and from behind every second door would come the shouting and the arguments over the issues of the day. Meanwhile the kids emptied out the local branch of the public library. "Have you started it yet?" That meant *Les Misérables* by Victor Hugo, a graduation of sorts. There was a rumor that it took six months to read. You went into training for *Les Misérables*.

Even the old folks were concerned with *education*. Your mother or your teacher dropped a bit of honey on the first book that was placed before you. You licked the honey to associate forever *sweetness* with *learning*.

Somehow, perhaps instinctively, the British novelist Ford Madox Ford understood all this. In 1926 he observed in *Horizon* that New York City owes "its intellectual vitality to the presence of the Jews . . . the only people in New York who love books with a passionate yearning which transcends their attention to all terrestrial manifestations."

I remember a song that would go like this in English (the words left untranslated are letters of the alphabet):

> By the fireside where the embers glow
> Through the wintry days
> There the teacher softly, with the little ones,
> Chants the *A-lef Beys*.

Learn your lessons well,
Remember, precious ones,
The letters of God's law
Chant ye once again and yet . . . once again
*"Kometz A-lef Aw"*

When you are older grown,
Oh, my little ones,
You will one day know
All the tender love and all the burning hope
That in these letters glow.


My Lord, our army is dispersed already;
Like youthful steers unyoked, they take their courses
East, west, north, south; or, like a school broke up,
Each hurries toward his home and sporting-place.

The quotation, of course, is Shakespeare's, from *King Henry IV, Part Two.* Shakespeare knew everything and remembered it all. Is there ever a release as jubilant as Friday's release from school? It is one of those single moments which is always new no matter how many times it recurs.

Going to school is the necessary ingredient for the jubilation. It is the release from discipline that creates the ecstasy. The boys "hanging around," our description of the dropouts circa 1910, never knew the exciting experience of school's letting out, and they were the poorer for it.

Much has been made of how children dislike school. I never remember disliking it on Monday morning. By Thursday there did seem many other things I would enjoy doing more. All of us on the Lower East Side of New York were quite well aware of how important school was, what promises it held forth. But these promises never offered immediate fulfillment, and we all said "Praise be" at 3 P.M. on Fridays.

Our joy was greater than that of the Irish and Italians. Friday afternoon not only began our weekend but our great religious holiday—the Sabbath. It is hard to re-create the reverence in which the Orthodox Jews of my boyhood held the Sabbath. Let me say the Irish and Italian boys had Christmas once a year, Easter once a year, and once a year a celebration on a saint's feast day. We had the same exaltation once a week, every week.

The Lower East Side was then the most populous neighborhood

Alla Nazimova as Nora in
*A Doll's House.*

in the world. Its streets were jammed with peddlers and neighborhood shoppers. Poor though we were, people were always
shopping, always bustling along the brick canyons. On Fridays,
however, there came a wondrous stillness. The streets were pa-
trolled then only by the Irish cops. The bearded men who held
the young boys by the hand had made their way to the synagogue.
Two blocks away from the synagogue that cop could hear the
muffled chant of the cantor and the murmuring of prayers by the
congregation.

Once the service was over, a boy came home to find his mother
in her one silk dress with a white scarf over her head.

At the Sabbath feast, a father told his sons how all the suffer-
ings of Jews through the ages were dedicated to this one moment,

the celebration of the Sabbath, God's supreme gift. And we all repeated the prayer:

> Praised art Thou, O Lord our God,
> Ruler of the Universe, Who has
> sustained us and preserved us and
> brought us to this day.

The Sabbath was the most important event in life. Preparing to become an engineer or a doctor or a writer or a salesman even was secondary to celebrating its arrival. Accomplishment was a bonus, as it were. Eventually, however, the bonus absorbed the joy of the Sabbath, which is perhaps as it should be. We knew and had proof positive that if we studied hard and kept going to school and reading books we could enter the American open society. It was a guarantee. The immigrant mother who couldn't speak English, told her children—this is America, the school is free, the library is free, the college is free. And then came the phrase I've mentioned that we all heard nearly every day—"In America you can become—an anything."

When the great waves of Jewish immigration landed, the newcomers knew nothing about baseball, football, or straight pool. For a whole generation their sport was talk. So the new principal of P.S. 20, Mr. I. Edwin Goldwasser, kept his classrooms down on Rivington Street open until midnight to give immigrants a place to argue. Nighttime music and drama critics, Talmudists, Zionists, Single Taxers, Socialists, Democrats, Republicans, and Tammany Hallniks lent the school an air of intellectual ferment and vitality that carried over into the classes I attended the next day.

Built in the 1880s, P.S. 20 has been closed down. But because it represented something more than a physical plant, a new P.S. 20, named in honor of the old one and for Anna Silver, mother of alumnus Charles H. Silver, former head of the New York Board of Education, in 1969 opened its double doors a few blocks east on Essex Street. In this brand-new P.S. 20 is a twenty-foot mosaic, unveiled at the dedication ceremonies, called the "Wall of Our Forebears." In it stand likenesses of famous P.S. 20 alumni—Paul Muni, George Gershwin, Edward G. Robinson, Senator Jacob K. Javits, Irving Caesar, and me, among others.

In those days, Jake Javits, like me, was a bookworm. Robinson was a good student, talkier than Javits. And it was Robinson, not

Javits, who was the politician. He was on the debating team; he organized the theatricals, collecting pennies for shows that cost a dollar or two to put on—a real chamber-of-commerce dynamo.

It was easy to know at school when lunchtime came. In the classroom we could hear a hot chick-pea vender out in front of the school yelling "Haiseh arbus!" We'd all run out and spend our penny on chick-peas heated over a galvanized stove shaped like a dresser drawer. Or we'd go across the street to a candy store we called "Cheap Haber's" where a penny would get two sticks of licorice, eight squares of butterscotch, or ten marbles.

The teachers used to discipline us with a ruler, a wallop on the hand. Then when you got home your father would whack you, too.

When a new immigrant boy speaking no English arrived at school we taught him dirty words to answer the teacher's "Good

A group of American Jewish actors in the 1890s.

morning." For this, when we got caught, came a mouthwash with soap. One Jewish mother complained about the practice, but only because the soap was made with pig fat. She furnished the teacher with kosher Sapolio "for the next time."

Old or new, however, P.S. 20 is more than a repository for the names of successful sons sprung from sacrificing mothers. P.S. 20 represents one of the most visionary experiments in the history of human relations.

The teachers of P.S. 20 not only taught American history but shared it. The first students in this school were German boys and girls, then came the Irish, followed by the Jews, the Italians, and the Poles. Each group took something away from the Lower East Side and each group left something there. Certainly the students in the new P.S. 20 at this time—mostly Puerto Ricans—will one day write a similar story.

## JEWS ARE NO LONGER A MINORITY

"It's a Protestant country," say the Episcopalians, Methodists, Presbyterians et al. And indeed it is a Protestant country if the Episcopalians, Presbyterians, Methodists, Baptists will count the Mennonites, Jehovah's Witnesses, the Seven Day Adventists as well as the Negro congregations—which the Methodists, Episcopalians, Baptists and Presbyterians do not often like to do. If they don't however, the United States becomes a Roman Catholic country because the Roman Catholics are the largest of all Christian denominations. New York is "a Jewish City" because the Jews by far are the most populous group of the middle class. But if the Negro, Puerto Rican, and welfare recipients ever escape the slums and dirty corners of New York, it is hard to tell what kind of a city it will be.

Jews own roughly 80 per cent of the small businesses. Small businesses are anything from a garment loft which cuts ten miles of cloth a year to a candy store near the public school selling four thousand pretzels over two semesters.

More than half the teachers in the public schools are Jewish, which is one of the reasons, if not the only one, why there is continual friction in the educational system. The Puerto Ricans want a teacher who may not even have attended college but who speaks Spanish to teach their neighborhood children. The Negroes want a soul brother. The problem will become more acute before it subsides.

A Jew in New York may not constitute one of the majority but he often feels he does.

The Irish cop knows what *meshpochah* means and Italian grocery stores sell Jewish rye bread. There are Oriental restaurants which advertise kosher cuisines.

The New York theater is Jewish, or at least its *milieu* is Jewish. This is not because the Jews have superior genetic arrangements for donning mask and buskin or because they are smarter producers. It's because Jews buy the tickets. Theater benefits were a habit developed by the immigrants on the Lower East Side. Local Hadassahs, fraternal organizations, and United Jewish Appeal (UJA) drives continue it. Jews attend the theater. They attend with the fervor a reformed drunk attends an AA meeting.

Producers do not bring in plays unless they have a big advance sale. Benefits insure advance sales. A sure way to book benefits is to produce musicals like *Fiddler on the Roof* or *The Rothschilds*.


## OUR ONE HUNDRED PERCENTERS


All our troubles, the nativists used to insist, could be laid at the door of the immigrant. The nativists were for "one hundred per cent Americanism," a phrase they borrowed from one of Theodore Roosevelt's speeches which, if it means anything, means that somehow those whose ancestors came here first were more American than those whose ancestors came later.

"One hundred per cent Americanism" has caused more division within the country than any Polish syndicalist or Italian anarchist ever dreamed of.

The Civil War Copperheads were 100 percenters. Eugene V. Debs was 100 per cent American when he opposed World War I and so was Woodrow Wilson who put Eugene V. Debs in jail. The brothers Berrigan are native-born patriots, no one contends differently, except their patriotism takes the form of pouring animal blood on draft board records. The Weathermen are native-born prototypes of the middle-class. They came from affluent families and went to college.

The Women's Lib Movement, which has induced all those little cuties to run around without brassieres, is not a foreign importation. My mother who did piece work as a seamstress and fed and clothed and cleaned house for a family of six plus a boarder and who went to the shul with a babushka around her head might have had a thing or two to tell Kate Millett and Betty Friedan.

Leonard Bernstein, former conductor of the
New York Philharmonic Orchestra and eminent
composer. His concerts for youth have been
a great inspiration to many young people.
Among his works is the classic musical *West
Side Story*.

Jan Peerce, Toscanini's favorite tenor.

Roberta Peters as Despina in *Così Fan Tutte*.

Richard Tucker, a leading tenor of the Metropolitan Opera as Radames in *Aida*.

# CHAPTER 2

# Where Have All Our Berthas Gone?

NOT SO LONG AGO I made a nostalgic journey through the streets of New York's Lower East Side. I stood in the doorway of our old tenement and looked at the flights of stairs my mother had climbed so often with her black leather market bag. I felt sad for a moment. I'd been back before a few times, but I hadn't really explored the neighborhood for nearly fifty years. There have been many changes, of course. The elevated structures of the Bowery and First Avenue are gone and there are a few new housing developments. But what is amazing is that so much of it is exactly as I knew it as a boy down there before World War I.

We lived at 171 Eldridge Street, a cold-water tenement house which must have been thirty years old in 1905. It is still full of tenants. Originally the toilets were in the yard in back. Later on came the inside toilets, one to a floor, serving four families. And I am talking about substantial families—father, mother, approximately five children, and three boarders.

I examined the names in the mailboxes of the tenement of today and where once there had been Rabinowitz and Cohen, there were now Perez and Figueroa. And as I stood in that hallway which had been my own for my first fifteen years of life, the Negro and Puerto Rican kids looked at me as if I had just dropped down from the planet Mars.

Before the waves of immigrants, in fact before there was a United States, the British lived here and they left us their names —Essex, Eldridge, Forsyth, Orchard, and Rivington. James Rivington was editor of the *Royal Gazette,* the leading Tory newspaper in the colonies. At the end of the rebellion, Mr. Rivington left for England along with the evacuating British army. The Americans, however, kept the street names eventually changing Rivington Place to Rivington Street. Whatever may have been Mr. Rivington's thoughts as he sailed away to England, he never imagined that one day on the site of his *Royal Gazette* would stand the Warshauer Shul built by an Orthodox congregation of immigrants in 1897.

You can write a social history of our country by walking through a neighborhood. First there were the Germans, then the Irish, the Jews, the Italians, and now the Negroes and the Puerto Ricans, and each group leaves its deposits for the future and stores away its memories. What manner of children, of what nationality and history, will be staring at the "stranger" when the Puerto Rican actor or Negro Vice President of the United States comes back fifty years from now for a visit to his place of origin? I am certain that this scene will be re-enacted over and over . . . "and in accents yet unborn."

The difference between the Indians of the American Southwest who lived in cliffs and the New Yorkers who live in apartment houses is that when the Indians came home from work, they left their dogs in the canyon below, to howl at the moon; New Yorkers *shlep* their dogs up by elevator to howl at the hissing radiators.

The Indians are only now coming into their own as a people with a viable culture which greedy white men wiped out. Their architecture was much more varied than that of the colonials or the immigrants. The Indians had a long house in New England, they had a round house in Florida, on the plains they invented the movable tepee as they quested for the buffalo and they had both the adobe house and the cliff house in Arizona and New Mexico.

Americans built cliffs wherever they built cities. The Indian was not, of course, plagued by the problem of how to realize the maximum from potential realty values which American land speculators were. If not civilized conduct, maximizing realty values is still an indication of the learning process. What the realtors did was to divide the landscape into grids whether the landscape accommodated grids or not. On top of these grids, of course, they threw up massive square diamonds of concrete, steel, copper, and, on occasion, aluminum. Where the Indian dreamed of the open

The mail boxes of 171 Eldridge Street. Sixty years ago the names on the letter boxes were Cohen, Rabinowitz, Levy. Today they are Perez, Rodriguez, Peralta.

171 Eldridge Street. A sentimental visit to where I lived as a boy in the greatest Jewish city in the world.

range which led to the Happy Hunting Ground, the American cliff dweller kept two different images traversing consciousness. The vision of America was the wagon train and the reality was the cubicle.

The red cliff dweller did not survive. Therefore, we can presume he was not happy. The white cliff dweller not only survives, but thrives, lending his techniques and joyousness to others. The symbol of the industrial age is the file cabinet, and the city cliff dweller inhabits the most extensive and complicated filing system devised. Even that Great Executive in the Sky couldn't find what he wanted in the cabinets of Chicago, New York, or even downtown Pensacola.

The cliff dwelling which I occupied, as you by now know, was on the Lower East Side of New York City. It was called the "dumbell tenement" because its floor plan resembled the weight-lifting dumbbell. It was six- or seven-stories high with two apartments of three or four rooms in the front connected by a narrow stairwell to two apartments in the rear. The latticing of fire escapes lent it a distinctive aesthetic touch.

I used to think we were exploited until I discovered the rich also lived in tenements they called "brownstones" which while roomier were equally as dark and airless.

Abe Cahan, who first conceived this metaphor around the turn of the century in order to explain the Indians of the Southwest to the Jewish immigrants, was of the opinion that cliff dwelling was an all-American tradition. All I can add is that the Indians had given up the cliffs around the time Cahan started to write.

I stopped on my journey at the University Settlement, of course, at 184 Eldridge Street. This is where Eleanor Roosevelt once taught dancing to the immigrant children. A few blocks farther west was the Christadora House, with its director Harry Hopkins. Lillian Wald, pioneer in public health nursing, organized a visiting nurse service in 1893 which provided free medical attention for indigent pregnant women and sent nurses to care for mother and child following confinement. Eventually this service became the famous Henry Street Settlement, where Mrs. F.D.R. also spent considerable time doing volunteer work. She was joined, in the early decades of this century, by other volunteer workers: Herbert H. Lehman, Henry Morgenthau, Jr., Frances Perkins, Gerard Swope, A. A. Berle, Jr., and Charles A. Beard.

The University Settlement House, in whose gymnasium I saw Eleanor Roosevelt teaching immigrant girls the Virginia reel.

I visited the Educational Alliance on East Broadway and Jefferson Street. I remember going there years ago to listen to Gustave Hartman lecture on Shakespeare. In 1908 and 1909 Gustave Hartman was the Republican assemblyman from the Sixth District. Samuel Koenig, meanwhile, was the second Jewish Republican leader in Manhattan, and Abraham Levinson, a Republican, was the first in the old Fourth District. In my youth I was a member of Clark House, at Rivington and Cannon, which had an extended basketball rivalry with University Settlement. Clark House basketball teams, light weight and feather weight, were tops from 1900 to 1906.

I went to Katz's Delicatessen store on East Houston Street, and surprisingly enough, Mr. Katz knew me. I had delivered some packages for him many years ago. I remember when the place opened; two newly arrived immigrants established it and they called it Iceland and Katz. Mr. Katz's nephew is the present owner. I never knew what happened to Mr. Iceland. It is a huge establishment today. I had a hot pastrami sandwich, pickle, and beer.

I looked up to the third floor of 173 Eldridge Street where lived my friend Morris Kaplan of whom I once wrote—the boy who created such a stir by going fishing every Sunday. And I stole a furtive glance down Rivington Street toward the corner of Forsyth to a low red building where Bertha Katzmann lived. Bertha was probably the most blue-eyed, blonde Jewish girl in the entire world, and every single one of us black-haired, brown-eyed boys felt his heart pumping away like mad every time we saw Bertha walking home from school. Her father was a violinist for the New York Symphony Orchestra, which, in addition to her rare beauty, gave her tremendous social status. When I was fourteen I attended some scholastic event at the 71st Regiment Armory, and looking up towards the balcony where the girls were singing, I saw Bertha waving that little American flag and singing, "The Stars and Stripes Forever." I have thought of that scene a million times during these past fifty-three years. Where is Bertha today?

Of course as we grew up into our teens we became aware of other girls in the neighborhood and eventually we took them out on dates, which was more or less a standard routine. On Sunday evening you took your girl to dinner at Lorber's Restaurant on Grand Street, where you enjoyed a memorable meal for twenty-five cents. (Sometime around 1912 Lorber's moved to Broadway across from the Metropolitan Opera House.) Then you went to the Plaza Music Theater at Madison Avenue and 59th Street to see a vaudeville show. The Plaza, which incidentally was in competition with Keith's, was run by William Morris, and on a given night we might see and hear Harry Lauder, Vesta Victoria (who sang "John Took Me up to See His Mother" and "There Was I Waiting at the Church), and other British entertainers. With or without a date, in those days I saw vaudeville acts that included the Avon Comedy Four (Cooper Brothers, Smith and Dale), the Arlington Four (three Jewish boys and a Negro), and Williams and Walker (the former later appearing in the Ziegfeld Follies). I saw McIntyre and Heath, black-face comedians; and Warren and Shean, who became Gallagher and Shean. At Tony Pastor's, which specialized in beginning vaudevillians, located on Fourteenth Street next to the old Academy of Music, I saw Lillian Russell.

I walked down to Seward Park and experienced a feeling of great warmth, and then I saw, still standing at the far end of the square, the *Jewish Daily Forward*, with the sign underneath, *Arbeiter Ring (Workman's Circle)*. In the old days we used to pick up our papers right on the sidewalk, two for a penny, and sell them for one cent each. I learned that I could dispose of the first batch quickly if I stood outside a few of the many meeting halls that were in session.

I thought of the *chazzer* (pig) market in Seward Park. Here the immigrants posted themselves with symbols of their trade, waiting for a casual employer to come along. One man held up his saw or hammer to indicate that he was a carpenter, one fellow carried panes of window glass, and others stood around with sewing machines strapped to their backs. (They called it "chazzer market" because the vendors were dirty and all were crowded together.)

At one end of Seward Park once stood P.S. 62. We were all jealous of P.S. 62 for its tremendous prestige in athletics. Its pupils were the first Jewish boys out of the Lower East Side to travel around the country playing in championship basketball tournaments. Eventually such distinctions became a tradition: young Jewish athletes went to Notre Dame for football, Holy Cross for baseball, and CCNY for basketball, the latter fed heartily by P.S. 62, where Nat Holman himself had been a student. The game of basketball was invented by Dr. James Naismith and

Lillian D. Wald, founder of the Henry Street Settlement. Miss Wald founded the Henry Street Visiting Nurses Services which eventually had branch offices all over New York, with district centers around New York City. She also inaugurated the first school lunch program. Her concern for the sick, the unfortunate, the young and the overcrowded led her to major involvement in almost every social reform of her time.

Her vision and courage has been largely responsible for the legislation resulting in the minimum wage, workers' compensation, the protection of women and children in the factories, and the abolition of child labor.

The above sculpture by Eleanor Platt was placed in the Hall of Fame for Great Americans at New York University on September 12, 1971.

the director of the YMCA, but the East Side boys made it a national pastime. It was the only game you could play in the settlement houses and schoolyards; and on every roof and basement you would see the barrel hoop with a flock of kids practicing shooting baskets by the hour.

There was the inevitable soul-searching one year up at Columbia University when it became necessary, according to leadership protocol, to appoint a Jewish boy as the captain of a varsity team. His name was Sam Strom. A year later, Dartmouth had the same "problem" and settled it with far more grace. There once was a player down on the East Side by the name of Moscowitz whom everyone called "Mosco." He played in an exhibition game up at the New York Athletic Club, which would not suffer a Jew to cross its threshold, and there they were, all the NYAC-niks standing on seats and yelling themselves hoarse—"Mosco! Mosco!"

We were spectator fans too. My favorite baseball team was the Giants, but we also attended the games played by the Yankees, who at the time were called the Hilltoppers or Highlanders and played at 168th Street and Broadway. A hospital complex now stands on the site of the Highlander games. We saw the Brooklyn team, known as the Superbas, play at Washington Park near the Wallabout Market in Brooklyn.

It was in Seward Park that William Jennings Bryan spoke (before my day) and where I heard Charles Evans Hughes deliver a campaign speech in his contest with President Wilson in 1916. It was in this district that a friend of my family was the assemblyman Judge Leon Sanders, a fine gentleman. The alderman was an Irishman by the name of Peter M. Poole. When he ran for re-election he plastered the district with Yiddish posters and called himself Pincus Meyer Poole. The Jews got the point all right and laughingly voted for the guy. Later John Ahearn became the leader.

Seward Park is now a city playground with a full-time director, a young fellow recently out of Brooklyn College who looks after the kids and supervises their play. Today the majority group is a toss-up between Negroes and Puerto Ricans, with smaller groups of Jews, Poles, Ukrainians, Italians, and a sprinkling of Chinese. I spotted the few Jewish boys in the park, who were undoubtedly Orthodox and probably going to a Yeshiva (religious school). While the little Puerto Ricans and Negroes had stomachs as flat

Room in a tenement
flat in 1910. Photo
by Jacob Riis.

as a board, these Jewish kids were literally bursting the seams
of their trousers. I made a prediction to myself. I said that the
mothers of these Jewish kids were watching them at that very
moment and soon would be coming along with a snack. Sure
enough along came a mother toward one of these boys with a
large paper cup full of a chocolate drink. Ah, "Ess ess, mein
kindt" (Eat, eat, my child). The old tradition never dies. I remember when young women practiced sitting postures to simu-
late a double chin, the mark of good health and good fortune,
which always prompted the remark, "She's so good-natured."

You were fifteen years old and you already weighed about one
hundred and forty-eight pounds, and if perchance you weren't
hungry one evening and dawdled over your supper, your mother
raised a terrible fuss: "Look at him, nothing but skin and bones."
Food, eat, eat. The tradition was born in the ghettoes of Eastern
Europe as both the symbol and the means of survival.

I walked, retracing old steps, toward the Williamsburg Bridge
at the foot of Delancey Street, and I thought of an awful incident
that had occurred to some of the early immigrants. It had happened a few years before I began to read, but it was still the talk
of the neighborhood. The Chief Orthodox Rabbi Ben Joseph had

passed away and the funeral procession was proceeding to the Grand Street Ferry while the Williamsburg Bridge was still under construction. As the procession passed the R. H. Hoe Company (printing machinery), some of its employees began to hurl discarded type metal down upon the heads of the mourners, and from one of the windows other workers turned on a hose, pouring out scalding water on the crowd below. Dozens of people were hospitalized. A riot squad of police ran into the building but could not properly identify the criminals. Before that day was over, every single window of the huge R. H. Hoe Company was shattered, with Irish cops helping to smash out the entrance of the building. In addition, the company suffered great loss through many lawsuits. There was no evidence to indicate that the owners and managers of the establishment were involved in the malicious mischief, but we all know that hate always brings on more hate and everyone suffers, including the innocent bystanders.

As my afternoon of memories wore on, it was time to enjoy a "for two cents plain" at a corner stand; only now it is for five cents plain.

The next stop was the establishment of the late Yonah Shimmel who invented the *knish* (a kind of pastry of either potatoes or buckwheat groats—*kasheh*—tenderly spiced and lovingly encased in a baked crust). I ate one of each—potato and kasheh. Mr. Shimmel's large photograph with his beautiful black beard is still in the window, and I wondered how he would have felt if he had known that someday his store would be advertising "cocktail knishes." As we get bigger and bigger in this world, the knishes get smaller and smaller. I was glad to see, however, that they still make *potatonik*, a potato pudding full of fine spices in a carefully baked brown crust. My mother made wonderful potatonik, although her real specialty was mammaliga, a soft corn bread. She cut it with a thread and you packed it full of sharp cheese; you could also use it with meat dishes to sop up the gravy.

Then I visited a clothing store—the kind where you could "buy a suit for Hymie," and I had a hilarious time. I talked to the storekeeper in Yiddish, telling him everything I had written about one of his earlier transactions. The fellow had a delightful sense of humor, patted me on the back and kept saying, "You remember, you remember."

I stood in front of the old P.S. 20, which is now the Manhattan Trades School. I went into that building every day for eleven long years, eight years to public school and three years to the East Side Evening High School. A few doors down stood the Rivington Street Library, gone now, where I read whole shelves of Verne, Hazard, Bulwer-Lytton, Dumas, Hugo, and later Emerson and Henry George.

I looked up to the top of P.S. 20. Ah, the old Roof Garden where Mr. Brown supervised the dances during the summertime. In those days the roof was brilliantly lighted and the entire neighborhood waited for the signal, the playing of "The Star-Spangled Banner." Our mothers sat at their windows just looking toward that Roof Garden. The immigrant milieu in America would never tolerate the changing of our anthem to "America, the Beautiful." We know. We are connoisseurs of America. We know that it is not the geography, but the *idea* of America that is important. The most beautiful "amber waves of grain" are in the Ukraine and in the Wallachian wheat fields of Romania; and I suspect that "from sea to shining sea" would be an appropriate description of many countries of the world. "That our flag was still there . . ." means something—the symbol of a great political experiment in human dignity.

Not far away—on Broadway at Ninth Street—was the building that once housed Wanamaker's department store, which for many

Backyard scene and a tenement building.

years was a symbol of a different sort for many of us. On the roof-top of Wanamaker's was a wireless station, and one night in 1912 this station received news that the *Titanic* had struck an iceberg and was sinking. Wanamaker's broadcast the news of this appalling event throughout the eastern seaboard on that fateful night, and as a result the United States Coast Guard was alerted for the reception of the survivors in New York Harbor. The operator who received and relayed the message that night was named David Sarnoff. And the station was a symbol of our neighborhood pride.

Finally my return journey's events came to a close with a dinner on Second Avenue in the establishment of Moskowitz and Lupowitz. In my day this was known as plain Moskowitz's and I remember how we sat outside at the curb listening to Mr. Moskowitz play the Romanian zither.

Street scene on the Lower East Side in 1912. Photo by Lewis W. Hine.

The steaks and roast beef covered wooden planks about twenty-four inches square, but after all, steak and roast beef can be had anywhere. No, this was no steak-and-roast-beef night for me. I started off with chopped chicken liver and a great big piece of radish. The chicken liver was of course well steeped in pure chicken fat. The waiter brought the ubiquitous bottles of seltzer. Then I had noodle soup with *kreplach* (the joy of which the late Senator McCarran did not fully understand) and then ordered a beautiful piece of boiled beef with a side platter of delightful stuffed cabbage—*holishkas*—which I worked on with a fork in one hand and a slab of rye bread in the other. For dessert I had compote—and a snifter of Three Star Hennessy brandy. All this time, of course, the three-piece orchestra was playing the delightful tunes of the Lower East Side, like "Leben Zul Columbus" (Long Live Columbus) and "A Breevele der Mamen" (A Letter to Mother).

I inquired about the original Mr. Moskowitz and I was amazed to hear that he was still living and actually playing his famous zither somewhere in Washington. How old could he be today? Of course he could still be under eighty, but he seemed close to middle age then; maybe it was merely the usual child's age-distortion of the adult world. Anyway Mr. Moskowitz was quite an institution. During the summer, whole crowds gathered outside his restaurant to listen to him play. His music was both soulful and wild. After each piece, everyone used to cheer and pour more wine, while Moskowitz, with his glistening bald head, bowed and bowed as though it were his debut, instead of the regular ten performances a night.

And so this was a day on the Lower East Side, and, with a bit of imagination, I could see my parents and my friends, and I could smell the smells, and I could talk with the parents and relatives of the thousands of people, all over America, who have been writing me all these years . . .

"We must have passed each other on the street."

# CHAPTER 3

# Come to Big Tim's Chowder and Pig's Knuckles Party

SINCE THE END of World War II, as I've said, the Jews have been moving out of the Lower East Side of New York City, and the Negroes and the Puerto Ricans have been moving in. Yet you'll still see thousands of Jews walking the streets of the old ghetto every day of the week. Many, of course, have remained in the tenements, particularly elderly people who feel comfortable there. Other thousands live there because they own stores or do business in the area.

Oddly enough, many Jewish young marrieds—artists, musicians, writers, actors, and directors—are moving from "uptown" into the heart of the ghetto in new government or labor-organization housing projects. They say the atmosphere is stimulating, reminding us of a David Riesman rule: "What the grandfather wanted to forget, the grandson wants to remember."

During a city-wide election you will see swarms of photographers and press agents following their candidate along these colorful streets. Their destination is either, or both, Katz's Delicatessen or Ratner's Restaurant. The candidate has come to be photographed eating *blintzes* and a kosher corned beef sandwich.

In our southern states political success once depended on which candidate won the race to "holler nigger" first. In New York it is a matter of which candidate wins the race to eat blintzes and a kosher corned beef sandwich first. I am convinced that Nelson Rockefeller beat Averell Harriman for governor of New York in 1958 because of this blintzes-corned beef gambit. Nelson was all over the place eating like mad. By the time the skinny Harriman woke up and made his move toward Katz's and Ratner's, it was too late. Too late and too little.

Three Jewish candidates for mayor, however, have been beaten badly by two Roman Catholics and a Protestant. The reason for this is that a Goldstein, a Lefkowitz, or a Beame impresses no one when he eats blintzes and kosher corned beef; what kind of occasion is that for celebrating? And the Jewish candidates can't quite make up for it by going into the Irish, Negro, and Puerto Rican sectors to eat ham or chitterlins or rice-and-beans. This would only make matters worse. This food is not Kosher and thus the Jewish candidate is forced to fall back on discussing the budget.

But off food and back to politics. When he was a newly elected Republican (now Democratic) mayor of New York City, the Honorable John V. Lindsay was more than gracious to me when I came to interview him. This, despite the fact that I had made speeches and written campaign literature for Abraham Beame in 1965, the Democrat Mr. Lindsay defeated. When he learned my purpose, Mr. Lindsay volunteered to have his top aides present. He said this with a twinkle in his eye, because we all knew his top aides were Jewish—Mr. Woody Klein, press secretary, Robert Price, deputy mayor and Harvey Rothenberg, the mayor's administrative assistant. Sanford Garelik would join his second administration. Mayor Lindsay told me that when he announced the names of his top aides, he received numerous letters, some simply asking, others angrily demanding to know, whether he himself was a Jew.

The interesting thing about the Jews in New York politics (and, for that matter, in America at large) is that until recent years they did not seek public office. At the beginning of this century they learned they could achieve equity by electing others. President William Howard Taft said, "The Jews make the best Republicans." Forty years later Adlai Stevenson said, "The Jews make the best Democrats."

For a long time only Jewish satraps of the political machines sought elective office. Politics did not attract the college-educated Jew. Instead he pursued a career in the professions, in medicine, dentistry, law, engineering, or in business. When truly outstanding Jews like Oscar Straus, Bernard Baruch, Louis D. Brandeis, Felix Frankfurter, Herbert H. Lehman, Joseph Proskauer, Samuel

Rosenman, Lewis Strauss, and Arthur Goldberg entered public life, it was because people like Governor Alfred E. Smith and Presidents Theodore Roosevelt, Woodrow Wilson, Franklin D. Roosevelt, Harry Truman, Dwight D. Eisenhower, and John F. Kennedy literally drafted them. And only in recent years have Jews of stature like United States Senator Jacob K. Javits decided to make politics a lifetime career.

The Democratic political machine of New York, which called itself Tammany Hall, established an equitable system for newly naturalized citizens. Tammany promised, "You Jews and Italians vote for us Irishmen and you'll have an equal share in the administration of the city."

This "equal share" was in the nature of what is called the "balanced ticket." The political offices, including the judgeships of the lower courts, were divided fairly among the Irish, Italians, and Jews, and, in recent years, the Negroes.

Mayor John V. Lindsay and three of his Jewish aides.

Big Tim Sullivan was the Tammany Hall power on the Bowery of New York. He was a tremendous man physically, and a tremendous man politically. He made a fortune out of his position as a Tammany district leader—principally from "concessions" to gambling houses and "Raines Law" hotels.

What was a "Raines Law" hotel? John Raines, a member of the New York State legislature, was a strict Prohibitionist who unwittingly established hundreds of brothels in New York.

Raines tried and tried, in the state legislature, to restrict the use of Demon Rum. Finally he succeeded in putting across a bill prohibiting the sale of intoxicating liquors on Sunday throughout the state, *except in hotels.* So what happened? Every saloon became a "hotel." The saloonkeeper knocked out a few walls upstairs and advertised rooms for rent. And what decent family would occupy rooms above a saloon? So pretty soon the rooms were rented out to prostitutes and the money just rolled in for everybody concerned (according to the Lexow and the Mazet investigations). The police got their share, the politician his cut; the saloonkeeper was able to buy a five-thousand-dollar pew in his church, and good old Mr. Raines had his "prohibition" on Sunday.

Big Tim Sullivan, who achieved power in the 1890s, was as colorful a character as ever wielded political power in this republic. During one of the periodic investigations which revealed some of his vast wealth. Big Tim made a speech to his constituents: "The trouble with reformers is that they don't know our traditions down here. They think just because I have a little money, there must be something wrong. I say 'to hell with reform.'" The crowd cheered. "And," continued Sullivan, "if I have done wrong, I have always thought I have done right, and I was always good to the poor." The women in the crowd wept openly and most of the men were dabbing their wet cheeks with handkerchiefs.

Big Tim gave us kids on the East Side a trip up the Hudson River to Bear Mountain every year.

Big Tim had about fifty student barbers working for him on every Election Day. These barbers performed a great service for Tammany. Along about August Big Tim sent word around the Bowery flophouses for the bums to let their beards grow. By Election Day, Big Tim had at his disposal several hundred Bowery bums, each with a full-grown beard. First, each bum would vote with a full beard under one name. He would then rush to one of

Sanford D. Garelik was elected president of the New York City Council, the second highest office in the city government, in 1969. Mr. Garelik had an illustrious career in the New York City Police Department spanning thirty years except for four years in the United States Army in World War II. His career culminated in his appointment to the highest uniformed detective position in the department, that of chief inspector. Mr. Garelik's courage and bravery won him six Police Department decorations, and at the age of thirty-four he was the youngest man at the time to achieve the rank of captain.

Council President Garelik, a registered Democrat, elected as a Republican-Liberal candidate, has been characterized as politically independent. As council president he presides over the City Council and has four votes on the Board of Estimate, as do the mayor and the city comptroller.

the stand-by barbers who immediately clipped off the chin fuzz. So then the bum with sideburns and mustache, looking like the Emperor Franz Josef of Austria-Hungary, voted under a different name. Then he would rush back to the barber and get rid of the sideburns; now, with just the mustache, he would vote for the third time. Finally the mustache came off and he would go out and vote for a fourth time—plain-faced, as Tammany called it.

For this day's work the bum got one dollar, three meals, a pint of whiskey, and of course a lesson in civics and good government, not to mention a free hair-cut and shave.

Big Tim and the other Tammany district leaders were careful to stay in the good graces of the foreign born. The Tammany sachems had henchmen roaming the districts looking for *bar mitzvahs*, weddings, fiestas, and funerals, but mostly funerals. The presence of the district leader at one of these functions made the voters very proud and they talked about it for years to come. "Just think, Patrick Divver, the leader, *himself*, was at the funeral of my father, God rest his soul."

Sometimes there was lots of trouble at these functions when

two Tammany factions were fighting each other, as often happened. Big Tim Sullivan, Tom Foley, and Patrick Divver attended all the funerals and christenings they could find. Each leader had a man stationed at the city-court clerk's desk to telephone whenever an Italian couple from the district came in to register for a marriage license. Each Tammany faction had a whole system of espionage to find out what kind of present the various camps were buying the couple. If the word went down that Foley was giving earrings to the bride, then Divver would give earrings *and* a set of cups and saucers.

Tammany leaders rarely made speeches. The henchmen went down the line getting out the vote and the "repeaters," and that was all that was necessary. Once, however, the Bowery congressman Tim Campbell did make a speech. His opponent in the race was an Italian named Rinaldo. Tim's only political speech was: "There is two bills before the country—one is the Mills bill and the other is the McKinley bill. The Mills bill is for free trade with everything free; the McKinley bill is for protection with nothing free. Do you want everything free, or do you want to pay for everything?

"Having thus disposed of the national issue, I will now devote myself to the local issue, which is the dago Rinaldo. He is from Italy. I am from Ireland. Are you in favor of Italy or Ireland?

"Having thus disposed of the local issue and thanking you for your attention, I will now retire."

Do not think for one moment that the Tammany men spent their own money on political campaigns. Campaign funding like everything else followed a system. They were uncouth, but not *so* uncouth that it showed to excess. These Tammany sachems could very easily relax of an evening at one of the fashionable university or millionaires' clubs on Fifth Avenue, during the course of which they might receive a big campaign contribution from a Wall Street tycoon, a traction magnate, a paving contractor, or a manufacturer.

The Tammany men in Congress and in the state legislature were in particularly favorable positions to deliver what they promised, because their constituency was composed mainly of "new citizens" who were concerned with one thing—survival. These new citizens were still struggling to gain a foothold in the new country, and if some politician helped along the way with a ton of coal at an opportune moment, or working papers for a young son, or

Bess Myerson, Miss America turned commissioner of Consumer Affairs. Her success proves that government can clean up the market place.

Bess Myerson is guardian of the interests of seven million New York City consumers and the implacable foe of dishonest merchandisers. She was named commissioner of the Department of Consumer Affairs of New York City on March 3, 1969. The department was a newly created one, the first of its kind ever organized in any municipality. Under Commissioner Myerson's leadership, it has maintained and extended its pioneering role in consumer protection.

Commissioner Myerson has been in the forefront of the consumer effort to achieve meaningful protection laws on the state and federal levels. She serves as adviser to the Senate Committee on Consumer Affairs and has presented her views and proposals to other congressional committees and to the regulatory agencies. Many of those views and proposals are now part of new regulations, new laws, and new amendments to old laws.

took the kids off the street for a boat ride, it was all right with them and certainly enough to get their votes.

This left the Tammany Hall politicians with complete freedom of movement in those economic and political areas which were not yet of vital interest to the voters in their districts. But it was a two-way street. The Tammany men were more sophisticated than they appeared to be, and the new citizens were not so naïve as they appeared to be either.

Tammany Hall Boss Dick Croker once told Lincoln Steffens: "Our people could not stand the rotten police corruption. But they'll be back at the next election. They can't stand reforms, either."

Croker was right. The voters of New York can get mad as hell over police corruption or scandal. They proceed to throw the rascals out—but after a little while they become remorseful and vote the machine back in with a vengeance. Once Tom Foley, a big Tammany district leader, was exposed as having banked a half-million dollars within four years on an aggregate salary of sixty thousand dollars. A year later he ran for district leader and was elected, with a bigger margin than ever.

The Jews were involved with Tammany Hall in politics, ideology, and economics. First was the fact that the Tammany Hall man met the Jew as he came to America and set up classes for him to learn English and become a citizen. Then there were the "benefits" Tammany provided for the immigrants of New York. These benefits included matzoh for Passover, a ton of coal when needed, jobs, housing, and getting Jewish boys out of trouble. The Jews were grateful to Tammany Hall. (Most of these benefits were later included in the Roosevelt New Deal and that was the beginning of the end of Tammany Hall).

In the old days the Tammany machine did a wonderful job for itself on Election Day. The joke went all over town, "Vote early and often," and it was much more than a jest. In the various flophouses on the Bowery the organization would gather hundreds of the bums and hangers-on, and as the vote was being counted in the various districts, those in charge of the bums would receive phone calls to the effect that such-and-such district needed two hundred votes and such-and-such district forty votes, etc. The phony voters would then be taken to the designated polling place, each armed with "credentials," usually the name of someone who, up to an hour before the poll was scheduled to close, had not shown up to vote.

Sometimes whole ballot boxes just disappeared. When the vote was going heavily against Tammany, the lights would suddenly go out and the ballot box would vanish. The vote tabulators, too, were sometimes provided with various devices, such as a ring

Charles Francis Murphy was for twenty-two years undisputed head of Tammany Hall. In a pre-election statement to the people he said: "If you Jews and Italians vote for us Irishmen you will each get equity." Tammany Hall maintained its power because of the "balanced ticket." If an Irish Catholic headed the ticket, a Jew was "number 2" man and an Italian was "number 3."

On the basis of the "balanced ticket," a young Jewish lawyer became a magistrate because it was raining. It was the night Tammany met to nominate three candidates for magistrate. They named the Irishman and the Italian, but when they called out the name of the Jew who was slated for the job, there was no answer. It was a night unfit "for man or beast." The fellow made a mistake in thinking that the meeting would be called off. An alternate name was called out; still no answer. Finally Charlie Murphy, the Tammany boss, a bit nettled, called out: "Is there a Jewish lawyer in the house?" A young fellow who had passed his bar examinations a few weeks before stood up. He was named magistrate. Turned out to be a darned good judge, too.

in which a piece of charcoal had been mounted. They palmed the ring and defaced the ballot, making it "void." In other instances, the "X" mark in the box had to be absolutely perfect, touching each of the four corners of the square—if it was for the opposition, of course. If it overlapped a millionth of an inch, it was marked VOID.

When Dick Croker became boss of Tammany in the 1900s he was a poor man. Some years later, Mr. Croker had an eighty-

Herbert Lehman was elected three times governor of New York State and twice to the United States Senate. When the United States entered the first World War, Lehman went to Washington as an aide to Franklin D. Roosevelt, then Assistant Secretary of the Navy. Later he was commissioned a captain in the Army and assigned to the General Staff in Washington. He was awarded the Distinguished Service Medal, retiring from active service in 1919 as colonel on the General Staff.

In 1928 Lehman was elected lieutenant governor on the ticket with Franklin D. Roosevelt who became governor of New York State. "America," Lehman said, "is a nation born of a great ideal and as long as the nation survives that ideal must be preserved and cherished." Within this framework, he said, "Jewish history teaches spiritual ideals in a people as well as in an individual, because strength and endurance transcend wealth and power."

thousand-dollar mansion and three hundred and fifty thousand dollars invested in race horses. It was a special kind of corruption. Mr. Croker improved on Boss Tweed's crude stealing and embezzlement. Instead, Mr. Croker engaged in what a New York police commissioner once called "honest graft." He merely padded the bills. In one year the city paid two hundred and eighty-five thousand dollars for letterheads and envelopes, and the cost of a courthouse rose to twelve million, four times the cost of constructing the British Houses of Parliament.

Charles F. Murphy, of my time, probably the greatest of all Tammany bosses, was interested in a company distributing a product known as "Rochester cement." The city building inspectors would inspect all new construction. No Rochester cement: ergo, a violation discovered. Naturally contractors bought Rochester cement.

Most of this sordid business, which occurs in each generation, was revealed first by the Lexow Committee in 1894 and again by the Seabury Investigation in 1932. But Boss Croker's basic political insight continued to apply. After sieges of reform the public would vote Tammany Hall back in again, time after time. After one reform administration, Tammany Hall ran on the platform: "To Hell with Reform."

During the Seabury Investigation, that brilliant old lawyer, Samuel Seabury, had Mayor Jimmy Walker on the stand for three days, and what Mr. Seabury was revealing, piece by piece, was a terrible story of graft, cynicism, and callous contempt for New Yorkers. Yet every question by Mr. Seabury was greeted with boos from the audience, and Jimmy was cheered after each of his answers. But Mr. Seabury was patient. It was in the Magistrates' Court that Mr. Seabury really hit pay dirt. It seems that some magistrates had paid for their position by putting up in cash an amount equal to one year's salary. In one night court where they tried prostitution cases, they had an established filing system. They arrested a girl, and she paid her fine. Then they put her card in a follow-up file, for use perhaps two months later, in order to give her a chance to earn sufficient money to "stand a pinch." It was revealed that, in putting in the "defense," a lawyer would say, "Your honor, there are one hundred reasons why this girl should be put on probation." The magistrate was thus tipped off how much was to be paid—one hundred dollars. If the papers in front of him showed that the woman had a long record and it was worth more he would shake his head slightly—and the lawyer would confer with his client and whisper, "Can you raise another fifty?" Then the lawyer would amend his plea and say, "There are a hundred and fifty reasons why. . . ."

Boss Murphy started his career as a streetcar conductor, then ran a saloon and quickly worked his way up to district leader. When he died he was worth a cool five million. Another big source of Tammany revenue, of course, came from selling legislation in the form of "contributions" from those who wanted a bill passed or defeated. When a Tammany governor, William Sulzer, defied Boss Murphy, the latter was so powerful that he simply proceeded to have the governor impeached in 1912. The "charges" against Governor Sulzer were meager, and he was destroyed only because he tried to introduce the direct primary in New York, which, of course, would have sawed the bosses in half. The amazing thing about Charles F. Murphy was that he could command the loyalty of good men. I am sure, for example, that wherever they are, the late Alfred E. Smith and the late Senator Robert F. Wagner are not particularly proud of the fact that, as members of the New York legislature, they helped impeach Sulzer. Sulzer was a dy-

Senator Jacob K. Javits, currently in his third term in the U. S. Senate and his twenty-sixth year in elective office, was born the son of immigrant parents.

Since 1946 when he first ran for Congress, the people of New York have given Jacob K. Javits an unbroken string of victories for the House of Representatives, attorney general of New York State, and the U. S. Senate.

Abe Stark, the president of the
Borough of Brooklyn.

Bella Abzug, the peripatetic
congresswoman from the Lower East
Side of New York. Mrs. Abzug has
been in the forefront of the civil rights
movement, won the Democratic
primary in 1970, and went on to win
over a Republican opponent.

namic speaker of the old school. I remember him well, traveling in an open car and waving a big black hat. He drank whiskey all the time, and to indulge this habit had developed an interesting system. He drank corn liquor, an unusual thing for a New Yorker, but this enabled him to take his quota in public. At an open meeting there was always a pitcher of water on the dais, with which Mr. Sulzer was refreshing himself. Corn liquor, of course, looks like water.

Tammany Hall was the most realistic organization in the world. It developed the knack of rolling with the punch. Thus, after a very bad scandal, it retired from the field for the moment by picking candidates "unspotted from the world." There was a calculated risk involved in doing this, but it was better than losing out entirely. Tammany took a chance that a high-minded, honorable candidate would eventually show his gratitude. But sometimes, as in the case of Mayor William J. Gaynor, he would sock Tammany on the head every chance he got. Occasionally, too, Tammany had to pay a political debt, such as allowing Mr. Hearst to pick himself a mayor. This Hearst mayor was quite a card. His name was John F. Hylan.

Hylan was an honest mayor, however, and there does not appear to have been much serious graft in his administration. But let us not get any wrong ideas. Boss Murphy was taking it easy. He was preparing to achieve his greatest ambition—to put a man in the White House—and during those years of grooming Alfred E. Smith, the rough stuff was suspended.

In one of the hot campaigns for mayor of New York in the old days, both sides used some interesting campaign posters. Tammany had refused to renominate Mayor Gaynor, and instead Boss Murphy picked one of his henchmen, a man by the name of McCall, to run for this great office. The anti-Tammany forces nominated a Fusion candidate, John Purroy Mitchel. Both sides were very eager to get the Jewish vote down on the Lower East Side and the Fusion people used a poster with a big headline, VOTE FOR MECHEL. (Mechel is a Yiddish name usually Westernized into "Max" or "Manny.") Tammany, not to be outdone, printed a photo-poster of Mr. McCall with the same headline, VOTE FOR MECHEL.

But pretty soon the sons and grandsons of the immigrants formed committees to send Tammany sachems to jail. But Tammany had been at it since Aaron Burr had founded the "Colum-

Arthur J. Goldberg was general counsel for the CIO 1948–55 and for the United Steel Workers of America 1948–61. Mr. Goldberg served as Secretary of Labor under President Kennedy 1961–62. President Kennedy appointed him Associate Justice of the Supreme Court on August 29, 1962. He was confirmed by the Senate on September 25, 1962, and took the oath of office and his seat on the court on October 1, 1962.

There are those among his friends who believe that the moment of his life that Arthur Goldberg regrets the most is the day he agreed to President Johnson's wish that he leave the Supreme Court to become the United States Ambassador to the United Nations. He was confirmed by the Senate on July 23, 1965, took the oath of office and his seat on July 26, 1965, and presented his credentials to Secretary General U Thant on July 28, 1965. He is now in private law practice.

bian Order of St. Tammany." It was a highly resourceful organization. Thus, when the new citizens themselves became aware politically, Tammany entered upon new schemes: alliance with gangsters and other resourceful measures.

Tammany has been in decline since the 1930s for several reasons. First of all, the constant population movement away from Manhattan to other boroughs of New York or to the suburbs has weakened the old stronghold of Manhattan, Tammany's power base. Second, the Fusion administrations of La Guardia in the 1930s and early 1940s drove Tammany underground. And finally the New Deal, which had political favors to bestow that overshadowed virtually anything offered by the old machine created new allegiances and alliances—and New Deal favors, remember, were administered honestly, which sometimes helps, even in New York City. In any case, it is no longer necessary for an Orthodox Jew to buy two five-dollar tickets to Big Tim Sullivan's Chowder and Pig's Knuckles Party at Ulmer Park.

# CHAPTER 4

# Where Are All Those
# Old Suspenders?

As a boy selling newspapers I used to walk along the most famous of all Skid Rows—the Bowery. In the early morning I saw the alcoholics still asleep in doorways and sometimes even stretched out on the sidewalk.

I can remember that the only people awake on the Bowery at 5:30 A.M. were the fellows opening up their saloons and cafés. They used to plaster huge signs in their windows, signs which read OATMEAL, 3 CENTS—WITH SUGAR, 5 CENTS—WITH CREAM, 7 CENTS. All over the Bowery were signs, BEDS—15 CENTS. And there were the usual missions with the big sign, SEEK SALVATION!

The clothing stores in the area employed husky fellows who stood outside on the sidewalk and pulled you in if you showed the slightest interest in the window display. This "pulling in" was an accepted custom, and a fellow confessed he was a "puller-in" as casually as someone would say he was a carpenter or plumber. Once you were inside the store, your chances of getting out without buying were very slim. If you took your pants off to try on a "new suit" you were a dead pigeon entirely. Unless you bought, your pants were suddenly lost.

Whiskey, known as "a stack of reds," cost ten cents; gin, "a stack of whites," was five cents; and beer, with a free lunch, was also a nickel. The fake auction store which you still see at seashore resorts, but with a few refinements, had its origin on the Bowery, with one in each block. One of the verses of the song, "The Bowery," describes them:

> I went into an auction store,
> I never saw any thieves before.

First he sold me a pair of socks,
Then he said, "How much for the box?"
Someone said, "Two dollars." I said, "Three."
He emptied the box and gave it to me.
"I sold you the box, not the socks," said he.
I'll never go there any more.

Less than seventy years ago most of the Jewish immigrants from Eastern Europe were peddlers, garment workers, and small merchants.

The first peddlers were New Englanders, fellows we describe in this more sensitive age as "white Anglo-Saxons," but who were then more generally called "Connecticut Yankees." Along about the 1830s this breed of New Englander had found a more desirable place as storekeeper and manufacturer in the growing eastern towns. There are dozens of cities in New England, like Meriden, Connecticut, "the Silver City," where silverware is manufactured, which became a city because it served as a peddler's headquarters, and as his trade expanded he hired other peddlers to help him while he spent all his time producing stock.

The Connecticut Yankee left the arduous peddling to the foreigners—immigrant Germans, a few Swedes, and, later, Jews: at first the German Jews, after the immigration of 1848; and after 1880, Jews from Eastern Europe—Russia, Austria, Poland, Romania, and Hungary.

Perhaps our popular chroniclers have paid little attention to the role of the peddlers in urban society because so many of them were Jews. The Jewish novelists, poets, essayists, and historians who wrote about America were understandably anxious to identify with the majority. Instinctively the immigrant grasped at the prevailing and popular values. To an immigrant a prize fighter deserves more respect than a peddler. So these novelists, poets, essayists and historians looked for prize fighters to glorify instead of peddlers. It is true that for every Jewish prize fighter, there were at least one thousand Jewish peddlers, but this was a statistic that did not concern them.

Despising the commercial man and favoring the romantic figure was not uniquely a habit of Jewish writers. Indeed, it is true of the majority of all American writers. Society generally—or at least the reader of popular fiction—holds the commercial man in some reservation, and he has rarely appeared as a hero in American literature. Sinclair Lewis, F. Scott Fitzgerald, Theodore Dreiser,

Henry Adams, Brooks Adams, and Henry James all expressed contempt for the businessman, his energies, and his values.

Dr. John P. Mallin in the *American Quarterly* (University of Pennsylvania) laid bare this phenomenon in a brilliant essay, "The Warrior Critique of the Business Civilization," in which he explained the rage American writers vent on the business culture. The Jews worrying about the anti-Semites who call them "Reds" today would be surprised to read the anti-Semitic literature published between 1840 and 1900. The anti-Semites were angry at the Jews for having "invented" capitalism. Brooks Adams, of that most noble American family, spent his old age in bitterness hating the Jews, writing that they had destroyed his world of knights, priests, peasants, and artisans by their creation of capitalism, which gave rise to the bourgeoisie. And then, ironically, with the assault upon "Jewish" capitalism, there is the identification of Jews with Bolshevism. The Jew carries the burden of history with him like a peddler carries his pack.

Jacques Maritain, the great Catholic scholar, reviewed the same point in *antisemitism* (Saunders, Toronto, 1959): "Like an activating ferment injected into the mass, the Jew gives the world no peace, he bars slumber, teaches the world to be discontented and restless as long as the world has not God; he stimulates the movement of history."

Furthermore, we know that a great-grandfather who fought with the Confederacy is a more romantic figure than a great-grandfather who simply supplied food to the Confederate soldiers. A grandfather scalped by Indians is a more romantic grandfather than one who labored building the railroads. Yet we also know that the sutler who carried bully beef to Robert E. Lee's troops served as significantly as the colonel who followed Pickett, and the grandfather who wielded a sledge hammer and drove countless spikes did as much for the United States as the grandfather who fired his last bullet at marauding warriors in his vain attempt to reach California. Good and bad men helped make America and so did romantic and pedestrian men. If there were pioneering wagon trains, so were there pioneering insurance companies and pioneering peddlers.

The peddler may be our forgotten pioneer, but two of the myths surrounding him are still current. The first is that he was dishonest, and the second is that he hoarded gold for the day when he would blossom forth as a merchant prince. The truth is that the peddler was never any more or less ethical than the rest of the mercantile civilization, from the days of the Venetian brokers to the cotton speculators of the 1970's. No doubt there were dishonest peddlers. But the vast majority were honest. Ultimately we must conclude this because merchandising of any kind cannot be consistently successful unless it is consistently honest. There were thousands of peddlers over the years who earned a livelihood at their trade, and that is virtually proof of fair practice.

The peddler invariably established for himself a regular route servicing the same people. Toward the end of the nineteenth century, he began to sell on credit, taking weekly or monthly payments, usually a pretty fair guarantee that the customer was getting what he paid for. The legend of the peddlers only emphasize their position as unassimilated aliens. They saved every penny, most of them, and gave their children a better chance than they had had. In turn, the children took care of the peddler father when he could no longer carry the pack. If there were no children, or if the children were poor themselves, the old gent would go to the Home for the Aged. He had insured himself for this security by paying monthly dues to one of the many self-help societies which the Jews had brought with them from the ghetto communities of Eastern Europe.

Why did so many immigrant boys and men take to peddling? Probably it was the quickest way to get started in America. The immigrant Jew could not speak the language of his new home. He was "different," too. He had little chance in the employment market. Therefore instead of "presenting" himself to the open society, he "presented" his merchandise. He felt by doing this he could learn the language and the ways of America and earn a living at the same time. And he could start earning the day after he got off the boat. Upon arrival at the dock he went to the home of a friend or relative, ate supper and gossiped for three hours, then got a good night's sleep. The next morning he went out and borrowed forty dollars from a different friend or relative and went down to the wholesale district. There he bought forty dollars' worth of sheets, pillowcases, and blankets and started walking toward New Jersey. A week later he was able to buy sixty-two dollars' worth.

The late Joseph Baumgartner, who peddled in the 1900s, told me stories of his "promotions." He would often introduce a new

Hester Street scene
in 1900.

An orange vendor
in 1895.

item of wearing apparel, a shawl perhaps or a decorative comb. He left the "exotic" item as a gift with two or three of his regular customers, who soon spread the word.

As a boy on the Lower East Side of New York between the years 1905 and 1920 I rubbed elbows with hundreds of immigrant peddlers—and patronized them too. On Orchard Street one could buy almost anything on the pushcarts—ladies' or men's shoes; men's trousers, shirts, and accessories of all sorts; household goods, eyeglasses, ladies' wear and accessories, and a multitude of miscellaneous items. People came from the far reaches of upper New York City to buy on Orchard Street; and tourists from out of town, those who knew the ropes, came too. In the early days, Grand Street from Orchard to the Bowery was a shopping center with more authentic shops and stores than crowded the curbs along Orchard. Lord & Taylor was on Grand and Chrystie Streets. And there was Ridley's, which had big stage coaches drawn by horses, no less, which picked up customers at the Grand Street Ferry on the East River and from the Desbrosses Street Ferry on the Hudson. Division Street between Orchard and Chatham Square was the ladies' wear center. The famous store there was Brenner Brothers, "A One Price Place," which meant no bargaining. Clinton Street from Houston to Grand was famous for ladies' millinery.

Thursday night and Friday morning were the bargain days at the big peddlers' market on Hester Street. Friday was also the big day for the Italian peddlers of olive oil, fruits and vegetables, and dandelion wine. The Italians peddled these foods, while the Jewish peddlers sold wearing apparel, umbrellas, and kitchen and household utensils. There was much fraternization and strong esprit de corps among the Jewish and Italian peddlers. Common poverty wove a strong bond of sympathy, and everybody understood that it was no shame to turn ingenuity toward making of a few extra pennies. The corner grocery fellow, for example, who was summoned to the counter when the opening door automatically rang a bell, added to his income by selling products prepared in his home, such as pickled herring, pickles, and sour tomatoes.

Chickens and geese, hung by the neck, were the great staples of the bargain market. You could buy a half or a quarter of a chicken. Many people who could not afford a whole one bought a few pieces for the Sabbath meal. After a while the health authorities transferred this trade in fowl from the streets to a special market close to the waterfront. At various points of the street, meanwhile, was the horseradish man, churning away at his machine. The last-named article was padlocked to a lamppost so it wouldn't be stolen when the horseradish man turned his back.

There were pack peddlers still making the rounds in the heart of the city, right into the fifth decade of this century. Some of these peddlers carried a load of 129 pounds, eighty-nine pounds strapped to the back and a forty-pound "balancer" in front. I remember fellows bent double under their packs, selling oilcloth, needles and thread, candles, and yard goods. Some of the yard-goods peddlers carried patterns with them, which they had received from their supply house to help push sales. For an extra three cents, a housewife could get a pattern for a child's dress or even for a Sunday dress or coat for herself.

What a business selling eyeglasses was in the 1880s and 1890s! So many bought eyeglasses that the peddlers became known as "glimmers." My father, who spent most of his eighty years reading books, bought a new pair of eyeglasses every year which usually cost twenty-five cents. He bought them from a peddler

Street scene, Mulberry Street, c. 1910.

79

who had a mirror mounted on his cart. The peddler also had a variety of daily newspapers—Yiddish, Polish, Hungarian, Italian, Russian, and occasionally one in English. His customers would stand around fitting themselves with eyeglasses, looking in the mirror to see how they fit, and picking up one of the newspapers to test the eyeglasses from all angles and distances. Seldom did the peddler fail to satisfy his customers, who often returned for a new "fitting." My father never had any complaints about his eyeglasses.

The peddlers who sold suspenders were legion. The suspenders dangled over their shoulders and down their backs. Apparently all of them made a living. I still wear suspenders, and I go into a store each year and get a new pair, even though the old ones are far from worn out. Which brings up the question: Why did so many men on the Lower East Side wear suspenders instead of belts? And where are all those suspender-wearers today?

Some of the pushcart and pack peddlers sold men's coats, slightly used. "As good as new!" they called. The price for each was fifty cents. The peddlers who sold pants, however, would take anything they could get for their wares. There were dozens of these fellows and they gathered in the middle of the street, many men surrounding them and fingering the pants, plucking at the seams. When a prospective customer walked away, dissatisfied with the goods, the peddler grabbed him by the sleeve and said, "Will you give eighty cents? Sixty? Fifty? All right, take them for thirty cents and make my Sabbath day unhappy." The buyer then took them for thirty cents and the Sabbath wasn't that unhappy either.

My classmate Yussl and I were ten years old, and he was helping his father at the pants pushcart. I can still recall the expression on Yussl's face as he listened to his father discuss a proposed purchase with a customer. He watched his father's every move, and how sad he was when the customer walked away without buying! The whole deal, of course, amounted to no more than a few pennies profit. Yussl would look up at his father with a reassuring nod, as if to say: "Don't worry, Poppa, we'll make a sale the next time!"

The rent for a peddler's pushcart was ten cents a day, and while most of the peddlers had regular stands, many of them routinely roamed the streets hawking their wares from the carts.

80

The peddlers carrying packs filled with candles and cutlery solicited inside the tenements, from door to door. There were also peddlers with the luxuries: nuts, fruits, chocolate, and candy.

I had another friend, a classmate, Harry Schwartz, whose father sold "broken" chocolates. These were big chunks of milk chocolate which he bought from a manufacturer as "rejects"—chocolates that could not be packed. Mr. Schwartz sold these irregular chunks for a penny a piece (he had a scale on the pushcart to weigh the larger purchases). I was visiting with my friend Harry early one evening, when his father came home. He washed, said his evening prayers, and sat down at the dinner table, but before he began to eat he called his wife and in lowered voice told her a story. A fellow buying two pieces of the broken chocolate had dipped into his pocket for the change, handed it to Mr. Schwartz and walked away. Mr. Schwartz opened his hand and there in his palm were two dimes instead of two pennies. He held out the two dimes and he and his wife smiled. I often think of those smiles and the two dimes when I pay $12.50 for a lunch for two in Charlotte's Tulip Room and figure I'm practicing Spartan thrift at that.

There were also peddlers with roasted sweet potatoes; two cents each, three cents for a large one. These peddlers pushed a galvanized tin contraption on wheels which looked exactly like a bedroom dresser with three drawers. In the bottom drawer were the roasting potatoes, in the upper drawers were the two different sizes ready to serve. Underneath all was the coal-burning fire. He had a small bag of coal attached to the front of the stove, and every once in a while he shook up the fire.

My uncle Berger once operated one of those sweet-potato pushcarts with the stove on the bottom, and years later he always said that he began life in America as an engineer. He boasted of this after he had made a million dollars operating the Hotel Normandie on Broadway and Thirty-eighth Street during World War I.

An interesting fellow was the peddler with a red face, a "Turk," who sold an exotic sweet drink. He carried a huge bronze water container strapped to his back. This beautiful container had a long curved spout which came over his left shoulder. Attached to his belt, in front, was a small pail of warm water to rinse his two glasses. The drink was one penny. You held the glass, and he leaned toward you as the liquid poured.

Pushcart scene on Orchard Street, the Lower East Side of New York.

Nuts were popular. There were pushcarts loaded down with "polly seeds" (sunflower seeds), and the Lower East Side literally bathed in the stuff. "Polly seed" was so called because it was the favorite food of parrots—"Polly want a cracker." The father of one of the kids on the block sold Indian nuts. On his pushcart he had a huge glass bowl the size of an army soup vat filled with nuts. I had daydreams of taking my shoes off and kicking my feet in that vat of Indian nuts, the way Harpo Marx kicked his feet in the peddler's lemonade in *Duck Soup.*

Shoeshine parlors were all over the place. On Sunday mornings you went out to get a shine and did not mind waiting in line for it either. "We are going for a walk next Saturday night." Sounds silly today, but it was an event then, make no mistake. And on every corner there were pushcarts selling fruits in season. Apples, pears, peaches, and, above all, grapes. A common sight was a boy and girl eating grapes together. The boy held the stem aloft as each of them pulled at the bunch and walked along the street. The grapes were sold by weight. In season, there was the man or the woman with "hot corn." I did not hear the term "corn on the cob" till many years later. We knew it only as "hot corn." The vendor had boiled the ears at home and usually carried the large vat to a convenient street corner or put the vat on a baby carriage and wheeled it around the neighborhood. A lot of women were in the hot corn business. Hot corn was a nickel, and there was plenty of bargaining. "Throw it back, give me that one, the one over there." We kids waited around until the hot corn lady was all sold out, except for the ones which had been thrown back, and often we paid no more than a penny for an ear.

Confections of all sorts were sold by peddlers. Fellows sold candy known as "rah-hott," which sounds Turkish or Arabic; it was a candy beautiful to look at and with two or three different tastes in each bite. Halvah, of course, was the big seller, and the memory of its taste has lingered with me to this day. No delicatessen store in New York today is without halvah, although I shall not do their owners the injustice of comparing the old East Side halvah with the packaged stuff they sell nowadays. But at least you do get a whiff of what it used to be like, which is worth anything you pay. (I had a Gentile friend in my present home town who had been courting a widow for years without any success till I gave him a box of chocolate-covered halvah to take to her. The candy was dandy. She said, "I do.") We used to eat it between slices of rye bread, "a halvah sonavich." A nut we loved was "buckser" (St. John's bread), imported from Palestine. It had a long, hard shell and inside a very black seed with an interesting taste which is hard to describe.

I remember some peddlers who sold only rainwear and umbrellas. And these peddlers did not always have to wait for a rainy day to make money. An umbrella was a mark of distinction. All the shadchens (marriage brokers) carried umbrellas, rain or shine, as a symbol of their profession. The rainwear peddler, of course, had his problems. His margin of profit was small and he had to be shrewd about the propitious time to replenish his stock. Some of these fellows were expert cloud readers who would probably score higher today in forecasting than the weather man on the late-night TV. But I remember one rainwear man who had an ingenious, somewhat mystical system that turned upon the cigarette sales of his brother, who ran a cigar stand. If the brother was selling cigarettes by the pack, it was time to buy more rainwear. If he was selling cigarettes singly, it meant stand by and wait. This peddler sent both of his sons through law school, so he was a forecaster of some merit.

I remember peddlers shouting, "Women, women, I need a 'first.' " I often accompanied my mother on her shopping expeditions to help her carry the heavy bags. In those days many of the peddlers kept stalls under the Williamsburg Bridge. As we were ready to go home, my mother would stop and say, "Go see if anyone hasn't had a 'first' yet." If I pointed to one of the stalls, my mother would make some token purchase there for a penny or two so that the man could have his "first."

Across the border (the Bowery) was the Italian hot dog man. The hot plate (a coal fire) was mounted on his pushcart, and behind the stove was a barrel of lemonade to which he added chunks of ice every few hours. The hot dog, roll, mustard, and relish was three cents; the drink, two cents; and the whole meal was a memorable experience.

A few years ago I saw a fellow with a similar cart near the Battery on Lower Broadway and I made a mad dash for him. The entire meal was now fifty cents, but it wasn't as wonderful as it was when I was twelve years old.

There were pushcarts then, as there were stores, loaded down with barrels of dill pickles and pickled tomatoes, which we called "sour tomatoes." Working people, men and women on the way home from the garment factories, stopped off to buy a sour tomato as an appetizer for their evening meal. These tidbits sold for two and three cents each. You put your hand into the vinegar barrel and pulled one out. Years later a relative of mine asked me to accompany him to a lawyer's office "to talk for him." I met him on the old East Side and we decided to walk out of the district and into Lower Broadway.

Suddenly I noticed that he was no longer at my side. I looked back and there he was biting into one sour tomato and holding a fresh one in the other hand, all ready to go. I had become a best-selling author by then and he was afraid his eating as we walked together would embarrass me, but my mouth was watering, Broadway crowds or not.

The pushcart peddler finished work about ten o'clock at night.

A man grinding knives was a popular visitor to the East Side streets at the turn of the century. He charged two cents to grind a set of knives and scissors and he made a living out of it.

When he got home to his tenement flat he placed his net earnings, probably $2.40, on the table. It was in silver and pennies. The mother waited up for him to share in the joy of parnosseh (livelihood) and the night of rest. If it is true that few peddlers got rich or even accumulated enough money to open a store, still nearly all of them were able to provide a better opportunity for their their children than they had had. Even in those early days there were many boys at the College of the City of New York (CCNY), whose fathers were peddlers.

But it was a hard, bare livelihood. The pushcart peddler contended against and was often victimized by the brutal police practices that corrupted the early years of this century. Every day the police made wholesale arrests, charging the peddlers with such misdemeanors as obstructing street corners, peddling without a license, or creating a public disturbance. To avoid these arrests, the peddlers paid extortion. These recent refugees from Jewish villages and ghettoes of Eastern Europe were asked to pay a surtax each month in the form of five one-dollar tickets to one of Big Tim Sullivan's affairs. If they balked, the cops ran them in and the judge fined them two dollars or put them in jail. There were peddlers who stayed in jail until nightfall because the fine was more than they could earn peddling that day. But most of the peddlers knew that while they were in court or jail, their pushcarts would be thoroughly ransacked.

This abuse came to an end when the newly elected mayor of New York City, William J. Gaynor, ordered discontinued the practice of making an arrest for violation of a city ordinance. Gaynor told the police henceforth only to issue summonses. And when the immigrant peddlers finally became citizens and organized the Peddlers Association, then it was Big Tim Sullivan himself who walked up five flights of tenement stairs to attend the bar mitzvah of the son of the president of the Peddler's Association. And Big Tim kept his derby on his head throughout the ceremony, in accordance with Orthodox ritual.

Yes, for a time the peddler's life was hard, but it also had its tremendous rewards. From these pushcarts have grown the huge wholesale fruit and vegetable businesses. Some Italian pushcart peddlers became great importers of spaghetti, olive oil, and other products of Italy. The Jewish peddlers became merchants, and now and then a former pushcart peddler has been introduced to an audience, justifiably, as a "merchant prince." At the same time, the peddler exemplified a pattern in business life that is as American as a Sunday-school picnic. That is to say, he practiced free enterprise in one of its purest forms. He had no help from anyone, except perhaps an initial loan from a relative who had preceded him to America.

The late Mayor La Guardia took pushcarts off the streets, city ordinances requiring merchandise to be displayed on the sidewalks, hugging the buildings for a certain number of feet. There was a great uproar when this happened, which La Guardia silenced: "Remember," he said, "you are no longer peddlers. You are now—merchants."

The peddler symbolized a belief and dedication to an idea. Recently I sat in the offices of an elderly New York lawyer who commands enormous fees and directs over thirty younger lawyers. We discussed the life on the Lower East Side that each of us had lived many years ago. In the middle of our conversation, this gentleman rose and went to his wall safe. From inside he extracted a small box and coming back to me with a smile, he opened it and let me look inside. It contained an old badge with the number 8721 on it—a pushcart peddler's license, issued to him in 1910.

The "customer peddler" sold an endless variety of goods to the immigrant and invented the installment plan. First he sold the immigrant a "shiff's carte"—a steamship ticket for the immigrant's relative. Because of this service, many immigrants did not have to wait years and years before they imported their immediate families, cousins, or brothers. The shiff's carte paid steerage class on the Hamburg-American Line. The steerage class ticket cost thirty dollars and the immigrant paid the customer peddler forty dollars at the rate of one dollar a week. The immigrant paid for the first few weeks, and then when the relative arrived and got a job, he took up the payments.

Steerage tickets were only a small percentage of the customer peddler's business. He made a profit on the sale of each steerage ticket, but, more important, with the arrival of the new immigrant he had himself another customer.

The first item he sold to the new prospect was a gold watch and chain. The watch and chain, the customer peddler explained, were the visible marks of an American and announced that the wearer was no greenhorn.

The customer peddler had the pick of the best boarders and relatives, the cream of the crop. Also he carried a whole line of engagement rings, earrings, curtains, and men's suits, to name only a few. An immigrant who found himself engaged to a girl, simultaneously found the customer peddler.

It is not hard to understand how the immigrant came to look upon the peddler as a sort of American "godfather." He was able to sell furniture to the *mochtunim* (the in-laws) and something to the *unterfuehrer* (who gave the bride away) to give to the couple as a wedding present. Quite often this present was a bed, and until the customer peddler delivered it, the newly wed couple had to sleep on a mattress on the floor. It was always called a "seven-piece bedroom suite," the seven pieces consisting of a frame, spring, mattress, bedding, chair, coatrack, and mirror. This too was paid for on the installment plan.

On his first day in America, my uncle arrived at our flat carrying an alarm clock in his hand. He had bought it from a peddler for $1.85, exactly five minutes after the immigration inspectors had cleared him for entrance into the New World.

Another unforgettable character, who deserves a section of this chapter all to himself, was the "hard-of-hearing" salesman, who flourished mainly in the men's clothing shops along Stanton Street.

Here is how he operated: A customer would be trying on a suit and every question he asked would have to be repeated three times. The salesman would cup his ear, distort his features, trying desperately to make out what the customer was saying— "What did you say? Please repeat it! I am very hard of hearing."

Finally the customer would pick a suit he liked. Now for that big moment. "How much?"

The deaf salesman would yell to the back, "Louie, how much for Number 2734?" And from the back would come the voice, very loud so the customer could hear it clearly, "Sixty-five dollars." The deaf salesman with a straight face would then turn to the customer and say, "Thirty-five dollars," whereupon the customer would pull out thirty-five dollars, grab the suit without waiting for the clerk to put it in a box and wrap it up, and hurry off with his "bargain."

Meanwhile Louie in the back room and the "deaf" salesman would go out to Davis's saloon to celebrate with a cold beer.

On nearly every corner was a soda water stand. These were the size and shape of the average newsstand you see in most of

Buying eggs off a pushcart on Hester Street in 1895.

the big cities today. There was a soda fountain behind a narrow counter, and a rack for factory-made American candy, becoming increasingly popular, especially the Hershey bar. The fellow also sold cigarettes. No woman was ever seen smoking a cigarette in those days. The brands were Mecca, Hassan, Helmar, Sweet Caporal (which are still sold), Egyptian Deities, Moguls, Schinasi, Fifth Avenue, and Afternoon.

My father smoked Afternoons. Half the cigarette was a hard mouthpiece, or what advertising today calls a filter. I bought many a box of Afternoons, seven cents for ten cigarettes. I also bought whiskey. There was no inhibition about it and no sense of guilt. We had no drunks down there, and a kid could buy a bottle of whiskey for his father as he could buy a loaf of bread. I read the label many times on the way home, "Pennsylvania Rye Whiskey; we guarantee that this whiskey has been aged in the wood twenty years before bottling; signed, Park & Tilford." Cost, $1.80 for an imperial quart.

The fellow with the stand almost always had a small marble counter on which he served his drinks and made change for candy and cigarettes. Along the counter were jars of preserves—cherry, raspberry, mulberry—for his mixed drinks. He also had a machine to make malted milks. How the immigrants took to the malted milk! Like the other folks, my mother pronounced it "ah molta."

But of course, the big seller was seltzer (carbonated water), either plain or with syrup. A small glass of seltzer cost a penny— "Give me a small plain." That meant no syrup. And for the large glass you said, "Give me for two cents plain." For an extra penny he ladled out a spoonful of one of his syrups and mixed it with the seltzer. Here, too, there was always bargaining. A fellow would say, "Give me for two cents plain," and as the man was filling the glass with seltzer the customer would add, casually, "Put a little on the top." This meant syrup, of course, and yet it did not commit the customer to the extra penny. It was all in the way it was said. Well, the man had already filled the glass with seltzer and what could he do with it unless you paid for it? So he "put a little on the top" but not the next time if he could help it. Often he would take the two cents first and give you a glass of plain. "I know my customers," he'd say. The man who had the stand on our corner was an elderly gent, Benny, and once when I was playing, one of his jars fell and the syrup spilled all over me. Every time I came near Benny's stand after that he took extra precautions. "Go way, hard luck," he always said to me. Benny wore a coat he had brought from Europe which reached to his ankles. He would take a handful of that coat, feel it a while and tell you whether it was going to rain the next day. People came from blocks around to get a weather forecast from Benny and his coat. He rarely missed.

Irving Caesar is one of America's all-time great song writers. His list of standard songs is staggering. He has collaborated on these songs with some of the most remarkable musical talents of the century, including George Gershwin, Vincent Youmans, Victor Herbert, Sigmund Romberg, Rudolf Friml, and Ray Henderson. The list is topped with such classic titles as "Tea for Two," "Sometimes I'm Happy," "I Want to Be Happy," "Crazy Rhythm," "Swanee," "Just a Gigolo," and "Is It True What They Say About Dixie?"

The composer Jerome Kern's first two successful musical comedies were *The Red Petticoat* and *Very Good Eddie*, the latter produced in 1915, which revealed him to be an extraordinarily gifted composer of popular music.

After that Kern wrote the musical scores of numerous successes, notably, *Sally, Sunny, The Cat and the Fiddle, Music in the Air, Roberta,* and the great American classic, *Show Boat.*

Irving Berlin, originally Israel Baline. For nearly half a century Berlin has been one of America's most prolific and successful writers of modern popular music. George Gershwin called Irving Berlin America's Franz Schubert. The son of an impoverished cantor who had brought his family to the United States in 1893 and settled on the Lower East Side of New York, Berlin wrote his first song, "Marie from Sunny Italy," in collaboration with N. Nicholson, while working as a singing waiter in a Chinatown saloon in 1907. His second tune, "Dorando," brought Berlin $25 the following year and a staff position with the Ted Snyder Music Company. He became a partner in the publishing house and later established his own firm. Berlin has written about 800 songs, which have earned him a fortune. Unable either to read music or to play the piano when he embarked on his musical career, the composer writes his melodies in the relatively simple key of F sharp, transposing with the aid of a specially constructed piano.

"Alexander's Ragtime Band" (1911), a pioneer among syncopated dance tunes, was Berlin's first nation-wide success. In 1918 Berlin was commissioned to write the music for the division review of Camp Upton, from which came "O! How I Hate to Get Up in the Morning."

George Gershwin's outstanding contribution to music, apart from his own work, was the elimination of barriers between one type of music and another. With his "Rhapsody in Blue" in 1923, he dispelled prejudice against the use of jazz or "popular" idiom in symphonic music.

His music is as unmistakably a product of this country as a George Bellows lithograph or a story by O. Henry.

Ira Gershwin, brother and partner of George, whose inspired verses blended perfectly with the composer's musical expression, making the two an amazingly well-matched musical team. Three satirical comedies, for which book and dialogue were furnished by George S. Kaufman, represent the most characteristic combined work of the Gershwin brothers in turning out scores of sustained quality, brilliant wit and constant variety of mood and color. *Of Thee I Sing,* most successful of the three, won the Pulitzer Prize in 1932.

George Gershwin's last and greatest work was *Porgy and Bess,* a folk opera whose book was DuBose Heyward's adaptation of his impressive play *Porgy* and for which Ira Gershwin wrote the lyrics.

# CHAPTER 5

# I Taste My First Drink of Grown-up Liquor

IRVING HOWE, in an article in *Midstream*, reminds us of the astonishing fact that in one fifteen-year period—from 1899 to 1914 —more than a million and a half European Jews entered the United States, most of them settling in New York's Lower East Side. Equally compelling are the interpretations Mr. Howe places upon this enormous modern resettlement. What did America mean to these immigrants? How did they adjust their lives from the style of the Old World to that of the New? What changes were effected in Jewish attitudes because of the transplantation? What shape did new institutions, activities, and values assume in the Lower East Side Jewish enclave, and what relationship did these new cultural patterns have to the old ones?

American Jewish life did not spontaneously spring into existence as immigrants stepped off the gangplank, but rather evolved by peculiar and unique combinations of Old World and New World experience. In its inability to shake off European habits and in its lack of readiness to adopt American values without question, the Lower East Side was obliged to improvise a world of its own. What emerged for a period of one generation was a momentary pause in a culture's normal forward progress, a brief transcendence of nationhood (the immigrant Jews were caught in between nationalities for a while), as the newcomers found means to adjust themselves and decide upon an identity and a sense of purpose.

One important feature of this new in-between existence was an almost unprecedented feeling of freedom of expression. In

Eastern Europe these Jews had been accustomed to circumlocution, cautious use of language both oral and written. In America they discovered that they could cry out to heaven without fear of the brutality or reprisal so traditional in European suppressive anti-Semitism. The result was a cultural fever on the Lower East Side, an epidemic of self-expression, vitality, and emotional liberation. Now the Jews could talk and argue, perform on the stage, lecture and discuss, read voluminously and defend their favorite authors, and tackle issues of a religious and philosophic sort that they had had to approach delicately a generation earlier in other countries. In this sense, the Jewish experience on the Lower East Side was a process whereby the Jews could express and unite their collective experience. New modes of life and thought were thereby forged, as in fact always happens when the members of any group open themselves to each other.

This experience was really a fulfillment of energies from the immediate Jewish past. What could not be said in Poland and Russia could now be said. Feelings and ideas and religious objections that had been long dammed up could now find release. But the important point is that there was no real break with the past, just an enlargement upon it and a development of it, a fresh

Steerage deck of the
S.S. *Pennland,* 1893.

expression and an evolution that accelerated when serious pressure was suddenly lifted.

Secular experience, for example, did not eliminate the Orthodox religious habits or explanations of morality. In 1898 Abraham Cahan in the pages of the *Daily Forward* not once but many times wrote about the Hebrew tradition for social justice: "Ours is a just cause. Saith the law of Moses: Thou shalt not withhold anything from thy neighbor nor rob him; there shall not abide with thee, the wages of him that is hired through the night until morning. So it stands in Leviticus. So you see our bosses who rob us . . . commit a sin . . ." Another sign of the continuity between the old and the new was the intense devotion of the immigrants to families and friends who were still in the Old Country. Many newcomers worked and overworked for years with no other purpose than to bring their relatives over for a permanent reunion. Because of this, in a way, for a decade or more Jewish immigrants seemed unable to focus their eyes on the immediate environment, glancing continuously as they did towards the regions they had left behind.

America and its influences finally ruled the Lower East Side, and the passage of time all but eradicated the habits and orientation which the immigrants had brought with them. This was so much so that many of the wiser immigrants began to fear this prospect and use the pun *ama reka*, the hollow people, to describe their feeling at the thought of a total loss of identity. This fear and this feeling are vividly enacted in Abraham Cahan's novel, *The Rise of David Levinsky*. Late in the book, when the hero is enjoying prosperity and status in the American style, he pauses to evaluate his achievements as a businessman, a Jewish Babbitt, and he tastes ashes. He is lonely. He doesn't relate in the old easy and familiar way to his friends—his riches embarrass them. He feels uncomfortable in his new clothes and he can't relax in his expensive apartment. He suspects that he will always have a lurking fear of the headwaiter in a fashionable restaurant. He actually yearns for the old days when he peeked in the windows of downtown delicatessens without the price of lunch or approached an East Side banker for a small loan to buy goods for the pushcart. Levinsky sighs, the causes of his unhappiness not quite clear in his mind, but certain that his past and present do not harmonize.

Despite this example, the Lower East Side should be judged

primarily as a vital, living creation, a warm, vivid reality that had much to contribute to the newly adopted homeland. What the Lower East Side achieved was a subculture known as *Yiddishkeit*, which is different from both the Orthodox culture and various secular ideologies, despite its strong connection with each. Yiddishkeit embodies a social and moral ethic emphasizing humaneness, affection, and discipline toward the young, commitment to improving things, and the idea of charity; all of these formed the foundation of the Jewish-American experience in its early years. Another of its great products was the intellectual worker, a type then rare in this country and rarer still in these days of "hard hats" and relatively uneducated rural workers coming to urban factories. The California stevedore Eric Hoffer is perhaps our leading contemporary example of this unusual combination of working activities and intellectual interests. But in the old days the Jewish workman could climb stairs to peddle his goods and at the same time look forward to reading Spinoza or Shakespeare during his lunch hour. Or he could work in a garment shop and mull over world history, politics, literature, and science. He was firm in the faith that knowledge was virtually a mode of redemption.

How long does it take to become an American?

I remember seeing the students come into the classroom of P.S. 20 two or three days after they'd left the boat. The girls had shawls, long woolen dresses, and black stockings and the boys in caps wore corduroy pants, the seats of which were invariably too tight. They were shy and afraid. By the next morning they had learned the Pledge of Allegiance and three weeks later they sat stiffly at their desks writing a poem about George Washington.

The schools on the lower East Side were brick buildings with iron fences around the playgrounds. You lined up outside doors marked BOYS or GIRLS and marched into your classroom.

On the first day of the fall term you had new clothes. They were usually handmade clothes, sewn together by Mother, and they were new in the sense that it was the first time *you*'d ever worn them. Very probably your brother had worn them last year and your cousin would wear them next. But all of us did get new pencil boxes each fall. These were flat, rectangular little boxes which cost a nickel. They contained three pencils, all sharpened, a pen and a pen point, an eraser, and a ruler, and sometimes, for older children, a compass. We also bought a new notebook every September with blue-lined writing paper. It was businesslike to walk to school with this efficient equipment. You felt there wasn't a fraction that couldn't be reduced or a sentence that couldn't be parsed. You had the tools.

One of the impressive facts of my education was that my first principal, Mr. Robert Smith, had lost an eye in the Civil War. What a thrill it was for us immigrant boys to read about the Civil War and to know that Mr. Smith had fought there, that it was not so long ago or so remote.

By the time he entered high school the immigrant boy was more deeply concerned with two other words—"working papers." You had to be fourteen years old to get the certificate—in order to get a job as an errand boy or a factory worker.

But everyone knew of a friendly notary public in the neighborhood who charged you fifty cents for working papers if you happened to be *under* fourteen. Perhaps this was out of order, but it was out of order on the side of America, and since it involved work, it also helped to enrich the human spirit.

Because the young immigrant boy was forever conscious that he was alien, he constantly looked into the faces of the Americans on the street and asked himself, "Ah, when will I talk like him, and when will I be like him?" And he did not have a moment to spare. He had to get on with the business of making good as quickly as possible. He couldn't wait till he was fourteen. He was worried about his accent, but he was sure that if he worked hard and studied hard, it was possible to hurdle an entire generation within a few years.

America turned the face of opportunity toward you in those days. That is why the immigrant mother, when asked, "How old are your children?" would reply with quiet confidence and dignity, "The doctor is four and the lawyer is two and a half."

A generation later she might have added the age of the school teacher, for today of the sixty-five thousand total teaching personnel who staff New York City's public schools, thirty-five thousand are Jewish. They have their own Jewish Teachers Association, which sponsors art programs and charter tours, handles complaints, and publishes a newsletter. There is at this time pressure for the introduction of Jewish history courses, Jewish-American history courses, and Hebrew language courses to be taught in the public schools—at least on an elective basis. No

Ellis Island, Immigration Bureau, in 1910. Every once in a while you'd hear a screaming woman. Inspectors might have discovered trachoma in one of her children's eyes which meant a separation in the family.

doubt this runs parallel to current demands on the part of American Negroes for inclusion of black history courses in our universities. Everybody, as Jimmy Durante says, wants to get into the educational act.

In the fall of 1970 Governor Rockefeller proclaimed a "Jewish Education Week" as a gesture to acknowledge Jewish educators' contribution to the advancement of learning and culture throughout New York City and New York State. "Jewish education has, over the years," said Governor Rockefeller, "brought to New York State the fruits of a proud heritage of learning, a history of scholarly achievement and a tradition of progressive educational involvement."

The history and the tradition mentioned by the governor are indeed realities, and the fact that they take different forms in different epochs only serves to remind us of their constancy. In Old Testament times the Jews already formalized learning. Teaching of the young was considered holy work. Wherever there were twenty-five boys, it was ordered that the community furnish a teacher; where there were forty, they had to provide a teacher and an assistant. Students attended classes from early in the morning until late in the afternoon, usually skipping lunch. Memoriza-

A young Russian Jewess at Ellis Island, 1905. Photo by Lewis W. Hine.

Inquiring, tireless, seeking
what is yet unfound,
But where is what I started for so
long ago—
And why is it still unfound?

Walt Whitman

tion was encouraged, as was reciting, even shouting and singing aloud to oneself. Childhood, it was thought, was the best time to learn. Teachers could strike a student only under severe provocation and if they injured the child they were suspended.

In these early schools Jewish boys learned ancient Hebrew and translated the Bible. At the age of ten they began the Mishnah (collection of laws). Later, science, mathematics, logic, and philosophy were included in the curriculum. In a sense, the story of Jewish education is the story of the Jews' survival through the ages, for it tended to fuse the community into a uniform and unbreakable unit, separate from the surrounding Christian milieu.

Throughout their history Jews emphasized and even bred for intellect—a direction which they chose themselves, but more often had forced upon them. In the Middle Ages, the Jews who wanted to marry and raise families were obliged to pay a fee to the city administration. The intention was to reduce the size of the Jewish community, but the effect was the opposite. Not only did the Jews flourish, but the wealthy class in particular increased. And, owing to the peculiar social conditions of the Jewish enclave, the well-to-do were mixed through marriage with the Jewish aristocracy of learning, resulting in a disproportionately high increase of population from the scholarly class. This tendency continued even during the centuries when European Jews were forbidden to practice any of the professions, but were permitted to deal only in old clothes, second-hand merchandise, and money-lending.

Persecution and pressures by power groups do not always lead to concentration upon intellect and learning among the persecuted, as it did with the Jews. The untouchables of India and the etas of Japan have merely acquiesced to society's decision to render them ignorant and powerless. But some unknown quality in the Jewish constitution, some drive or instinct, remains forever active. This quality might be simply an innate genetic characteristic.

Today the Jews represent 3 per cent of the population of the United States. They constitute 6 per cent of the college enrollment. They comprise 9 per cent of the membership of Phi Beta Kappa, the national scholastic-excellence fraternity. In the Directory of American Scholars, Jewish representation is approximately 70 per cent higher than the national average for other ethnic groups. According to recent editions of American Men of Science,

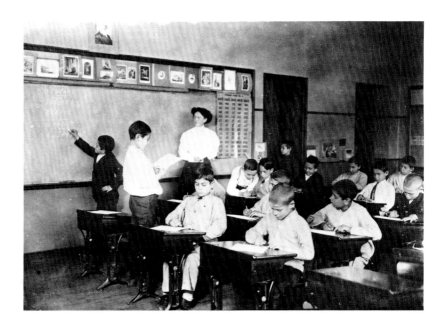

Classroom, 1910.

Jews contribute twice as much knowledge and activity to the physical and biological sciences as would be the statistical expec- tation. Jews comprise approximately 20 per cent of the profession of psychiatry and psychoanalysis in America, perhaps because Sigmund Freud, the founder of psychoanalysis, was a Viennese Jew.*

My mother used to sigh and say that life was perhaps more pleasant and prettier back in her native village, but that no Jewish boy there, no matter how smart, could go any higher in professional life than apothecary. The crowded tenement, she said, was worth the agony. The thesis that immigrant experience was a fulfillment of long-held Jewish cultural traditions rather than a completely fresh start has some merit and degree of truth. But it is an idea too retrospective, too centered in the past. The fulfillment of the New York immigrant Jews lay not in their past but in their future. Life on the Lower East Side was exciting, vital, enormously stimulating. But instead of a glorious termination in Jewish history, it was a transition to something better.

The years between 1908 and 1918 were the years when girls wore what we called bicycle stockings and boys did not put on their first pair of long pants until they were seventeen or eighteen. I worried about when I would get my first long pants. I worried and longed for them because my ambition was to go into a saloon, and you did not pass through those swinging doors unless in long pants. Finally the great day came when I shed my "knickers" and straightway made for the brass rail. I was nervous. I stood beside a fellow at the bar and listened carefully to what he ordered. "Birch beer," he said. "Birch beer," I said. Birch beer tasted like Seven-Up. My first taste of "grown-up liquor" was a soft drink.

Women's dresses came to the floor. Magazine advertisements were already urging women, however, to wear silk stockings because some of the dresses were short enough to reveal ankles. My sister had stockings which were silk past the ankle and lisle the rest of the way.

Horses and carriages constituted the main traffic through the street, although we saw occasional motorcars. The Dubrows, the one rich family on the block, owned a car, a Winton. I studied

* Statistics and related information about the Jews in academic and professional life are taken from *The Creative Elite in America* by Nathaniel Weyl, Public Affairs Press, Washington, D.C. (1966).

this car with the other kids while Mr. Dubrow made his rent collections. Finally, one day, we could bear the suspense no longer and we prevailed upon his chauffeur to come out and lift the hood.

The Broadway theater was booming. I was one of the few boys on the Lower East Side who knew something about it. My brother was a night clerk in a Broadway hotel and I visited him often. The greatest thrill in my life at that time was to spend all night Friday in a theatrical hotel on Broadway. The biggest electric sign in the world blinked on and off advertising the play *Ben Hur.* This was soon superseded by the Wrigley's Chewing Gum sign.

Second Avenue, sixty years ago, was the main street on the Lower East Side, a miniature "Great White Way." It was the promenade for young people, and every Sunday afternoon resembled the Easter Parade on Fifth Avenue. The main Jewish sport was to take a walk. Here and there while walking you saw a German coffee house left behind when the Germans moved out of the neighborhood generations before and on a corner you could occasionally see an Irishman polishing beer glasses, stubbornly hanging on to his saloon.

And now all over the districts were the Jewish tea houses, Jewish fraternal halls, and the synagogues.

Where Second Avenue meets Houston Street was the famous National Winter Garden where the Jewish artists played, later to become a burlesque house; and on the corner of Fourteenth Street was the Labor Temple, organized by the Presbyterian preacher Charles Stelzle, where I heard Margaret Sanger and Dr. Will Durant. And coming into prominence about this time were halls and "mansions" for the social functions, bar mitzvahs, weddings, and dances. The big apartment houses already accommodated those East Siders who had done well but wanted to remain in the neighborhood. We kids used to pass these apartment houses and read the glamorous names over the main entrances. The apartment houses were not "171 Eldridge Street" as were the apartments in which we lived but had names like the baronial mansions in Europe. The Imperial was one, and the Victoria Hall and the Trianon, the last named after the winter palace of King Carol I and Queen Elizabeth ("Carmen Sylva") of Romania. These swell apartments were populated by Jewish politicians, bailbondsmen, and lawyers whose business came out of the neighborhood.

The folks who made good in the professions, in industry, and

in commerce, however, left the neighborhood. They moved uptown to Washington Heights in Manhattan, or to Flatbush in
Brooklyn, or to the Bronx. This was the pattern followed by my
family, from the Lower East Side to Vyse Avenue in the Bronx,
where in 1918 we could still see the goat farms.

Sixty years ago it took you four hours to go from midtown
Manhattan to Queens, where Kennedy Airport is today. You had
to change trolleys three times and you always missed one and
had to wait another half hour.

Social life on the Lower East Side?

The ladies of the ghetto were never "at home," but the welcome
visitor was always sure of his glass of tea, his dish of preserves,
and some fruit. There were no *Kaffeeklatsches* here, no progressive
euchres, or bridge-whists. Hospitality was simple, homely, and
genuine. Parties were given; not coming-out parties, but engagement parties, graduation parties, bar mitzvah parties. The wedding, of course was the big function. Hundreds of societies gave
dances and receptions (the latter being simply a more pretentious
name for the former) during the winter, to which anyone could
come if he could pay the price of a ticket and hat check. Some
societies coupled entertainments with these receptions. The great
social events were the entertainment and ball of the Beth Israel
Hospital, the Hebrew Sheltering House and the Home for the
Aged, the Daughters of Jacob, the Young Men's Benevolent
League, and the Hebrew Orphan Asylum, founded by Gustave
Hartman, a school teacher who became a successful politician.
It was at these functions that the Lower East Side made its most
gorgeous sartorial displays, and they were by no means either
crude or cheap displays. The women for the most part were as
well dressed as the ladies who visited the Horse Show. The dia-
monds worn at these affairs could be outblinked only by the
collection on the grand tier at the old Metropolitan Opera House.
The East Side was not all poverty and suffering.

Owing to home conditions on the Lower East Side, there was
only such social life for the young folks as was made possible by
organization membership, at the dances mentioned above, or in
open meetings, sponsored by the literary societies, Zionist societies, and clubs in the settlements. In the summer time there were
picnics—dances in an open pavilion, with a few patches of grass
surrounding it, all enclosed with a high fence.

The Russian Jew was not a teetotaler, but neither did he need the solicitous guardianship of a temperance organization. He drank when he felt so inclined, or when it seemed to him the occasion warranted it. Of course, there had to be a reason to justify a drink, and a good reason too. For example, there was always gefilte fish on Sabbath eve and Sabbath lunch. Not to have a little brandy before the fish course, during the fish course, and after the fish course—that would be to desecrate the joy of the Sabbath! Then there were the festive occasions, the "Rejoicing of the Law," the anniversary of the hanging of Haman, the celebration of the Maccabean victories, and the miracle of the lights—surely, these were sufficient reason for looking upon the wine when it is red. Then, too, the great family events: the *birth milah* (circumcision), the *pidyon ha-ben* (a ceremony relating to the first-born), the *bar mitzvah* (thirteenth anniversary of a male child), the *tnoyim* (engagement), the wedding—surely one could not invite friends to these great functions without previously having a small keg of beer brought in. People cannot sit at a dry table!

But drinking on these occasions was done in the house. The Jew did not lean on the bar, nor did he sit in the saloon. If he liked a glass of beer with his meals, he had a bottled supply on hand.

For all this, the favorite drink of the Lower East Side was tea. Tea served in the coffee saloon—which was the East Side's favorite place for recreation and intellectual stimulation. Whether to play chess or checkers, to discuss Karl Marx or Bakunin, to analyze Tolstoy or Ibsen, to debate the relative merits and demerits of the naturalistic drama, to admire the coloratura at last night's performance of the Metropolitan Opera, to denounce the critics of Adler the actor, or to excoriate the traducers of Gordin the playwright—it didn't matter. All dialogue was expanded best in the coffee saloon, where words poured and thoughts flowed over a glass tea *à la russe*—that is, with a floating slice of lemon—and an aromatic cigarette in hand.

While we're on the subject, let me not fail to mention the marvelous Jewish Cookery of New York. The type of cooking which is known as Jewish has developed gradually as a result of the combination of dietary laws, festival customs, and historical influences. Specific dishes differ widely not only in preparation but in use, so that a food which is popular among Jews whose ancestors came from one part of the world is utterly unknown to other Jews. With the nineteenth-century emigration from Eastern European countries, however, the dishes which were most in use by the Jews there have become the most familiar in Jewish settlements everywhere. They constitute the basis of modern Jewish cooking, though variations and exceptions still remain.

The festive meal on Friday night is not the result of any special regulations, but has grown out of the command to celebrate the glory of God on the Sabbath. Besides, many of the Jews in Europe were traveling artisans, apprentices, and petty traders who returned home only for the Sabbath, frequently having had little food during the week. The usual courses of the Friday night meal in those Eastern communities which were transferred as customs to the new world were gefilte fish, soup, and roast meat or chicken. The bread is *challa*, a white loaf, which signified a holiday in the European communities because it differed from the black bread which was the daily fare. It usually was baked in a long twist, sometimes flavored with saffron, painted with the yolk of egg to give it gloss, and sprinkled with poppy seed or *kimmel* to represent the manna which came down in the desert.

Kreplach are bits of chopped meat enclosed in small three-cornered bits of dough and cooked in soup. They are considered holiday fare among the Jews, perhaps because they require effort and time to make; and the expenditure of effort and time on food signifies luxury. On the day before Yom Kippur it is as much a requirement to eat well as it is to fast on Yom Kippur itself.

Chanukah, which comes at the beginning of the winter, is generally identified with the eating of *latkes*, or pancakes. These may be potato pancakes, made of grated potatoes mixed with egg and fried, *matzoh* meal pancakes, or any other kind. For the eating of pancakes there is no definite explanation. The custom may have arisen because the Chanukah season produces no new specialty, and at the time of its observance it is hard to obtain fruits.

Purim is today most usually associated with *Haman taschen*. Haman taschen are three-cornered cakes made of sweet dough thickly filled with poppy seed, raisins, or prunes. Honey is sometimes also painted on top of the cake before it is baked.

Blintzes seem to have a Russian-Polish origin. They are made as follows: first a thin pancake made of fine batter is fried. Into moderate-sized pieces of this thin dough the cheese, mixed with egg, is wrapped. Then the blintzes are either fried again until

A Jewish immigrant established in a dismal coal cellar of a ghetto on the Lower East Side of New York preparing for the Sabbath. Note the challa on the table. Photo by Jacob Riis.

brown, or baked. They are spread with cinnamon and sugar or sour cream.

During their sojourn in the western periphery of the Mediterranean the Jews seem to have acquired eating habits which they carried with them into the remote parts of the Continent and finally out again into the Western world. The foods easiest to obtain and cheapest to buy are the ones that remained in the Jewish diet. This may be why the cookery commonly called Jewish today is known for its heaviness. It is not really because the prohibition against the use of milk and butter with meat keeps the balance toward the heavy side, but because the cheapest fare, the fare of the lower classes, is in every country of a fundamental and heavy nature. The Jews have accumulated unto themselves many such national diets.

*Kishka* is stuffed intestine. Bread crumbs or flour, fat, and minced onion constitute the stuffing. It is boiled or roasted with the meat.

*Knishes* are made of mashed potatoes enclosed in a thin dough and baked.

*Pirogen* has been taken over from the Russian diet. Cooked meat, liver, or lung is mixed with minced onion, rolled in dough, and baked into small cakes. This is served as a side dish with soup.

Chopped liver is a lower-scale adaptation of *pâté de foie gras.*
Not only goose liver, but chicken liver and even beef and calf
liver go into the making of it. Onion is added, sometimes a hard-
boiled egg. It is used as an hors d'oeuvre everywhere.

Among the many Jewish institutions of New York City, the
eating places loom large in tradition and contemporary significance. In Manhattan you have Isaac Gellis, Ratner's, and Stein-
berg's. In Brooklyn it's Dubrow's and Garfield's, both opulent
cafeterias which are always open and which cater to a large variety of Jewish Brooklynites.

The sign painted on the side of Garfield's reads THE CAFETERIA
OF REFINEMENT: ESTABLISHED 1912. But the decor inside, faded
mosaics and piers done in the style known as Art Moderne, which
was a streamlined version of Art Nouveau, clearly announces that
the latest renovation was completed sometime in the 1930s or
early 1940s. Garfield's stands on the corner of Church and Flatbush, across the street from the Reformed Protestant Dutch
Church, which has a plaque that reads THE FIRST CHURCH IN FLAT-
BUSH WAS BUILT UPON THIS SITE BY ORDER OF GOVERNOR PETER
STUYVESANT IN 1654. The church, however, occasionally closes its
doors to the faithful. Garfield's never does.

A good many high school students eat lunch or after-hours
snacks in Garfield's. They come from nearby Erasmus Hall High
School, and the girls dress in bell bottom pants suits, while the
boys wear body shirts and fringed vests and have long hair.

But the deep-down faithful population of Garfield's is the old
Jewish ladies and the old Jewish men, for whom the faded glories
of the once-glittering cafeteria are a home away from home. One
old lady is actually known to live there. The mailman understands
and drops off the mail to her at the seat near the window on the
Flatbush Avenue side. When relatives want to see her, they go
not to her home but to Garfield's. Once years ago, she faced a
crisis. Around midnight in April of 1948, they closed up Garfield's
for a thorough spring cleaning. Aunt Luba, for that is what everyone calls her, was in a panic. A friend came by in a car, however,
and solved the problem by taking her to Dubrow's, which is a
place very much of the same cut, for the remaining hours of the
evening.

Old men shmooze and old ladies doze in Garfield's.

The menu reads "Stuffed pepper"—"Potato pancakes"—"Danish
pastry."

In recent years Garfield's has become a hunting ground for Jewish widows seeking new husbands. "Can I borrow your horseradish?" a little old lady asks shyly of a middle-aged customer who has just seated himself with a cup of coffee to enjoy a solitary half hour. The question seems innocent, but watch out! It conceals a deadly intention. Good-bye, solitary coffee sessions in the cafeteria! Another famous romantic ploy is to hang around the self-service food line and wait until a likely looking prospect comes along. Many an unsuspecting old bachelor or widower has been caught off guard at the bagel counter. By the time he reaches the chopped chicken liver he is holding hands. When he gets to the chicken soup, he's a goner. By the time he reaches the cheese blintzes, they're engaged. The cashier could easily double (but does not at this writing) as a justice of the peace. A friend of mine years ago wrote a poem in honor of Garfield's. It is entitled *Kubla Kohen* and it goes like this:

> In Bensonhurst did Kubla Kohen
> A stately cafeteria decree
> Where Gowanus, the sacred canal, ran
> Through caverns measureless to man
> Down to the BMT.

Of course Garfield's is not in Bensonhurst, and the Gowanus runs nowhere near it. But what's the difference? The spirit is all that counts.

Meanwhile the old folks snooze and shmooze in Garfield's, the Jewish Xanadu.

The two great indices of a national character are always reflected in sport and art. Art because it is so self-conscious and sport because it is so unself-conscious. A man may write good poetry because he has conscientiously studied the great poets or because he has hit upon his own unique voice. But he goes to the ball game because he played it as a boy or because by going he can be himself. In sports a man, or for that matter a nation, can be utterly honest and open. In Philip Roth's *Portnoy's Complaint*, the rebellious young son finds almost no point of contact with the values of his father's generation—except in one scene, when he watches them playing softball. At that point he is overcome with respect and admiration.

On the Lower East Side we did not play soccer; there was no space in the city streets for that game. We had heard of it of course; it was known as "Gaelic football," and the Irish teams played occasionally in the Polo Grounds. But for us the game held no interest.

Neither did we play much baseball. We played a variant of it, called stickball, with a broom handle and a five-cent rubber ball. The diamond was from fire hydrant to fire hydrant, and the manhole cover in between was second base. Today the kids buy brightly colored commercial sticks for this game, but the spirit of the original remains. The man at bat throws the ball in the air and wallops it without benefit of pitcher or catcher. He then runs lickety-split for first base and tries to make it back to home be-

Sandy Koufax, the greatest strike-out artist in the major leagues, the only man to pitch four no-hitters.

111

fore the outfielder pegs it to the infielder and puts him out. The true essence of the game is in economy of the number of participants. Three, possibly four players is the rule, and each man is an entire team in himself. One of the hazards is careless selection of that first-base site. Many a young player has skidded into the gutter after tripping over a sewer opening.

Anyway, on the Lower East Side stickball did not produce many great baseball heroes for the big leagues. Sid Gordon and Hank Greenberg were great Jewish ballplayers, but the Jews generally never produced a Babe Ruth or a Willie Mays. But they did produce a great pitcher who has won election to the Baseball Hall of Fame. Consider Sandy Koufax. When a Jewish boy from Brooklyn, the greatest strike-out artist in the majors, pitches a night ahead of his turn so that he can observe Rosh Hashanah the next day—and on that night, with his Dodgers tied for first place with the Giants, ten games to go to decide the pennant, hurls a perfect game, facing only twenty-seven Cubs in a 1–0 victory, millions of fans, despairing or rejoicing with every pitch —then Jews can truly say they are part and parcel of the American experience.

Sometimes we played ring-a-levio and Johnny-on-the-pony.

We also were great handball addicts. We played constantly, using the side of a building until the janitor or the cop on the beat chased us off. Today all over New York City the kids still play this game, using a pink rubber handball put out by Spalding and officially called Hi-Bounce by the company. But to the kids it's a "Spaldeen," and that's what they call the game as well. When I was a boy we had two varieties, Chinese and American handball. In Chinese you hit the sidewalk first; in American, the ball bounces off the wall first. Or maybe it's the other way around. Anyway, reports have come in from various universities that New York City handball has metamorphosed into a thing called "mailbox ball" in some of our more exclusive universities. Required is the kind of set-up where mailboxes are cubbyholes built flush into the wall of a lobby or corridor; then look out! The rubber handball is constantly bounding off the floor onto somebody's letter from dear old dad.

The Jews on the Lower East Side primarily produced boxers and basketball players, and probably for the same reason—both boxing and basketball are indoor sports. Nat Holman and Benny Leonard are two names that still ring a bell. We also turned out

The Statue of Liberty. This world-famous statue has been the symbol of freedom and hope for millions of immigrants. It is 151 feet high and stands on a pedestal of about the same height.

The center of the Lower East Side of New York. Down these streets marched several million immigrants to America. On the corner of Rivington and Eldridge was P.S. 20 and across the street was the University Settlement.

Katz's Delicatessen where the candidates for governor and mayor come to eat blintzes and corned beef sandwiches.

The Warshauer Shul on Rivington Street, the site of James Rivington's Tory publication.

A small chapel of Shearith Israel Synagogue on Central Park West.

The Bedford Avenue Synagogue (Orthodox) which once was the Holy
Trinity Lutheran Church.

Another house of worship that changed identification as waves of newcomers
to New York succeeded each other. The Church of Jesus Christ which was once
a synagogue.

The ethnic melting pot of modern day Williamsburg.

In the Williamsburg section of Brooklyn, the Mea Shearim of the United States, little Jews look like their forebears in Eastern Europe and receive the same traditional religious education.

Temple Emanu-El (Reform), the largest Jewish house of worship in the world.

On the façade of the Temple Emanu-El on Fifth Avenue.

The ornamentation of the Torah is done not only as an end in itself but often is a necessary means of protecting the valuable and precious Scrolls of the Law.

The Torah is enshrined within the ark.

An elaborate silver Torah case.

Orchard Street, Lower East Side. Once the customers were all Jews. Today they are Puerto Ricans and Negroes.

The garment center in New York, where the sidewalks are full of shmoozers and the streets are full of trucks.

The Garment District.

The Solomon R. Guggenheim Museum, designed by Frank Lloyd Wright, one of the leading tourist attractions in New York City. The museum was founded by the Guggenheim family.

The interior of the Guggenheim Museum.

The greatest Jewish city in the world.

a few football players who were invariably passers. On the city streets you faded way back and lobbed the old ball high and far down the canyon so that the receiver could outrace the bus as well as the other team's cover. This is the way Sid Luckman worked it anyway.

A good many older men who grew up in New York are trying to introduce stickball and handball into Israel—without success. The Israelis want to know why they should bounce a ball off an apartment building when they have a wide open countryside available for soccer. The old-time New Yorkers have tears in their eyes, but the Israelis know what they're doing, just as the East Side boys knew. They are making the best of what they have.

I have read where the kids of New York today play a Franz Kafkaesque game called "judge," indulged in to initiate a new kid into the neighborhood or to get even with one who is unpopular. A few players are selected to go out and round up the "robber," who then stands trial before a judge and jury. The charges are trumped up and there is no defense possible. The offending boy is guilty no matter what. Then the others throw vegetables at him, or anything else that comes to hand. Whew!

We never indulged ourselves in scapegoat games of this sort. The Romans weeded out most of the Jewish Zealots in the Great Revolt of the first century A.D. Meanwhile we had our books, stickball, Caruso records, school, ring-a-levio, handball, and the whole teeming adventure of Life on the Lower East Side.

CHAPTER 6

# Our Houses and
# Habits of Worship

As THE JEWISH IMMIGRANTS moved into the Lower East Side of Manhattan and Brooklyn's Williamsburg, the Irish and Germans, who had lived there for several generations, moved out. But when they left, they had to leave behind their cemeteries and churches. The lighted cross of St. Mark's Lutheran Church dominated the entire East Side.

After a while many of the churches were sold to make way for one more tenement. Occasionally a church was acquired by a congregation and refurbished into a synagogue. The Bedford Avenue Synagogue formerly had been the Holy Trinity Lutheran Church.

Today the process continues, but in reverse. On a street now occupied by Puerto Ricans stands the Church of the Holy Name of Jesus—formerly a synagogue. And tomorrow? New York City's changing houses of worship are an index to the never-ending adventure of Americanization and its mobility.

Today there are approximately 4,380 organized Jewish congregations in the United States. In New York City there are 1,094 Orthodox congregations, with slightly over 400 buildings; 98 Conservative congregations with 53 buildings; and 100 Reform congregations with 70 buildings.

John Miller's map of New York in 1695 pinpoints the Mill Street Synagogue. The Mill Street Synagogue housed Congregation Shearith Israel which is now in its fifth edifice on beautiful Central Park West and Seventieth Street.

Indeed, all the Jewish life of New York for over a century and

Map of Lower Manhattan, 1744, in the days when all the Jews owned was the Mill Street Synagogue.

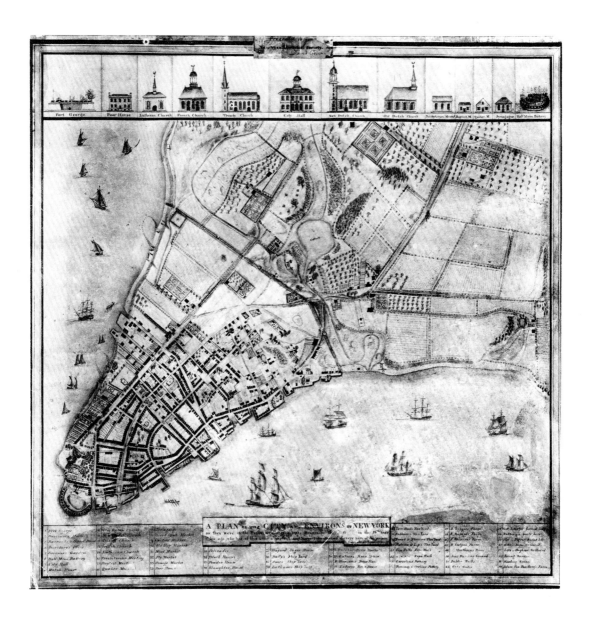

a half in colonial and early America centered around the then Sephardic* Congregation Shearith Israel, of which Gershom Mendez Seixas was rabbi (1768–1816).

The first Jewish school in New York City, Yeshibat Minhat Areb, was founded in 1731 by Congregation Shearith Israel. Reorganized at the beginning of the nineteenth century as the Polonies Talmud Torah, it was subsidized by public funds and conducted for half a century as a parochial school with a curriculum including English, reading, writing, arithmetic and Hebrew. Toward the middle of the nineteenth century the Polonies Talmud Torah became an afternoon weekday school supplemented by a Sunday school.

Portuguese was used in the congregational minutes until 1736. English gained the upper hand after 1736 because many of the congregants were native-born colonists who spoke the language of the mother country. By 1757 Shearith Israel was seeking a *chazzan* (cantor) "to teach children Hebrew by translation into English."

Even in this early period there were notable examples of interfaith co-operation. A number of Jews subscribed to the construction of a steeple for Trinity Church in 1711, and Gershom Mendez Seixas was particularly friendly with the Episcopalian ministers of New York. Frequently Seixas was invited to address Christian congregations, and members of the latter were supposed to have visited Shearith Israel. In 1789 Seixas preached a Thanksgiving Day sermon, and in that same year he participated in the ceremony inaugurating George Washington. In 1784 he was made a trustee of Columbia College and served in that position until 1815.

For more than three centuries, Congregation Shearith Israel has been intimately identified with the history of New York.

The present building was erected in 1897. In the cornerstone, laid in 1896, there are Jewish ritual articles, some earth from the Holy Land, and much historical information. The cost of the building exceeded $250,000, an impressive sum in those days. At

---

\* *Sepharad* is the Hebrew word for Spain and *Ashkenaz* the word for Germany. Sephardim are the Jews who came from the Mediterranean countries; Ashkenazim, the Jews who came from Central Europe and Russia. The rituals of the Sephardic congregation differed from those of the Ashkenazic. But they did not differ in their belief in one God or in the Prophets of the Old Testament. The Sephardim were the first Jews to emigrate to America. Not until 1820 did the Ashkenazim follow in any significant numbers.

the dedication on May 19, 1897, the doors were ceremoniously opened by Dr. Horatio Gomez, a great-great-grandson of Lewis Moses Gomez, president of the congregation when the first synagogue on Mill Street was dedicated.

The building, of Greek Revival style, was designed by the noted architect Arnold Brunner. In the north entrance hall there are two massive millstones, five inches in thickness, dating back to a mill erected in the latter part of the seventeenth century at the place where Mill Street became Mill Lane. These were brought to the synagogue in 1894. These stones recall the mill above which the Dutch Church of Manhattan held its services from 1628 to 1633.

Shearith Israel keeps a separate gallery for women, the traditional separation in Jewish houses of worship since ancient times. Even in the earliest days of the congregation in New Amsterdam this evoked no comment from Dutch Reformed neighbors, who also seated men and women separately. Tablets set up in the L. Napoleon Levy Auditorium pay tribute to the memory of Amelia Barnard Lazarus Tobias "whose beneficence knew no creed" and Sarah Lyons, principal of the Polonies Talmud Torah School of the congregation from 1898 to 1934.

To assure that the reader's words will carry, the reading desk is set near the center of the synagogue. So that present congregants can stand in prayer where their forefathers stood, the floor boards came from the reading desk in the Nineteenth Street Synagogue, to which they had been brought from the Crosby Street Synagogue of 1834, and, it is said, originally from the Mill Street Synagogue building of 1730.

Three of the Torah scrolls in the Ark, rescued from the Nazis, come from the Sephardic congregation in The Hague. The oldest pair of bells crowning the scrolls bear the Hebrew date 5497 (1737). Another pair bears the name of Myer Myers (1723–95), a well-known New York silversmith. Two of the pointers used in reading the Torah are inscribed with the date 1846, although others may be older. The beaten brass lamp kindled during Chanukah may well be two hundred years old.

The four lamps hanging on the eastern wall of the synagogue were rededicated in 1921 to the memory of four men of the congregation who gave their lives in World War I. Along the western wall of the synagogue auditorium are a number of memorial tablets. One of these, affixed in 1905 on the two hundred and

SHEARITH ISRAEL SYNAGOGUE IN THE CITY OF NEW YORK
MILL STREET
1730 - 1817

The Mill Street Synagogue known as Shearith Israel which is now in its
fifth edifice on Central Park West and Seventieth Street. (See following
pages.)
Jewish life of New York for over a century and a half in colonial and early
America centered around the then Spanish-Portuguese (Sephardic)
Congregation Shearith Israel.

SHEARITH ISRAEL SYNAGOGUE IN THE CITY OF NEW YORK
MILL STREET
1818 - 1833

SHEARITH ISRAEL SYNAGOGUE IN THE CITY OF NEW YORK
FIFTY-SIX CROSBY STREET
1834 - 1859

SHEARITH ISRAEL SYNAGOGUE IN THE CITY OF NEW YORK
THREE WEST NINETEENTH STREET
1860 - 1896

Shearith Israel today Central Park West and Seventieth Street.

fiftieth anniversary of the congregation, commemorates the ministers, as the rabbis were then called, from Saul Pardo, who came to New York from Newport in 1685, to Jacques J. Lyons, who died in 1877. Two other tablets, originally set up in the Crosby Street Synagogue, honor Abraham Touro, "whose practical efforts to cherish the religion of his fathers were only equaled by his munificence which showered his blessings without sectional distinction," and Washington Hendricks, another philanthropist who was one of the supporters of the congregation. Another tablet in the L. Napoleon Levy Auditorium below the synagogue recalls Hendricks' "liberal bequests to the Ladies of the Association for the Moral and Religious Instruction of Children of the Jewish Faith."

The Little Synagogue which abuts the main synagogue is a colonial chapel. It is a composite of the synagogues occupied by Shearith Israel for more than three centuries under the Dutch, the British, and, since 1783, the United States.

A plot of land on St. James Place was the Chatham Square Cemetery of Shearith Israel. A plaque over the gateway to the cemetery has the following inscription:

> This tablet marks what remains of the first Jewish cemetery in the United States consecrated in the year 1656 when it was described as "outside the city."

The tablet refers to the cemetery that was located on a plot of ground granted to the Jews of New Amsterdam by Peter Stuyvesant in answer to a petition by Abraham de Lucena, Salvador Dandrada, and Jacob Cohen Henricques.

On the northeast corner of Fifth Avenue and Sixty-fifth Street is Temple Emanu-El (Reform), the largest Jewish house of worship in the world and probably the most beautiful. The German Jews, who had preceded the Jews from Eastern Europe by two generations, built this temple, which is influenced by the basilica structure common in Italy. The exterior walls are of variegated limestone. The dominating feature of the exterior is the great recessed arch on Fifth Avenue, enclosing the rose window with its supporting lancets and the three entrance doors. On the exterior the motifs of the carved decorations have been drawn in general from Hebrew symbols. The symbols of the Twelve Tribes of Israel appear on the front of the temple and Bible verses in Hebrew characters appear on the front of Beth-El Chapel, which adjoins the main temple on the north.

The Reverend Dr. David de Sola Pool, the late rabbi emeritus of the Congregation Shearith Israel. The first rabbi of the Congregation was the Reverend Gershom Mendez Seixas, a patriot of the Revolutionary War and a trustee of Columbia University. Another was the Reverend Dr. H. Pereira Mendes who ministered to the congregation from 1877 to 1937. Dr. de Sola Pool came to Shearith Israel Congregation in 1907 and was the minister until the time of his death in 1970.

In studying the Freidenberg Collection of Medals of Jewish Historical interest, Edna Fuerth Lemle, political scientist, took steps to commission a relief of Rev. Dr. de Sola Pool. Dr. Pool's medal was struck in celebration of his eighty-fifth birthday. The medal depicts Dr. Pool in his rabbinic robe with the seal of the de Sola family at the right. The de Sola seal belongs to one of the most ancient families with a recorded history in the Sephardic world, going back to the ninth century in Spain. After 1492 branches of the de Sola family migrated to Portugal, Holland, England, South America, the islands of Central America, Canada, and the United States. They were among the pioneer families of the western hemisphere.

Temple Emanu-El is across the street from the House of Living Judaism, the seat of the Jewish Reform movement in America. In its ten stories it houses the headquarters of the Union of American Hebrew Congregations, the National Federation of Temple Sisterhoods, the National Federation of Temple Youth, the New York Federation of Reform Synagogues, the World Union for Progressive Judaism, the National Association of Temple Educators, and the offices of the Combined Campaign for American Reform Judaism.

Congregation B'nai Jeshurun, 270 West Eighty-ninth Street, is one of the seven oldest existing Jewish congregations in the United States. It was established in November 1825, as an offshoot of Congregation Shearith Israel, by a group of English and Dutch Jews who wished to follow the Ashkenazic rather than the Sephardic ritual. In a letter to the trustees of Shearith Israel, these Jews wrote: "We find it difficult to accustom ourselves to what is familiarly called the Portuguese Minhag, in consequence of our early impressions and habits . . . the increase of our brethren is so great and in all probability will be much greater in a few years, that accommodation, particularly on holy days, cannot be afforded to all . . . the great increase of New York and the distance situation of the Shool renders it necessary to have a new place of worship in a more convenient situation for those residing up town."

Among the founders of B'nai Jeshurun were John I. Hart, son of the Reverend Judah Hart of Portsmouth, Rhode Island, and Abraham Mitchell, one of a handful of Jews who served in the War of 1812.

The Eastern European immigration after 1880 put Orthodox Judaism in the forefront. In 1870 there were seven Orthodox shuls in New York, of which only two had buildings. By 1914 there were three hundred and fifty Orthodox congregations with over one hundred buildings.

Actually, by numbers and influence, the Jews of New York are still primarily Orthodox. And the twentieth century has seen great strides, such as the establishment of Yeshiva College, of some eighteen smaller yeshivas, of forty-one Talmud Torahs, of hospitals, old age homes and orphanages under Orthodox auspices, and the great efforts by the Orthodox Jews during this century toward establishment of a Jewish state in Palestine.

Yeshiva College was established in 1928—the first college of

First Jewish Cemetery in New York, south of Chatham Square.
It is designated as a Landmark of New York under the
supervision of the Cities Trust.

Congregation B'nai Jeshurun commemorates its 140 years as the
oldest Ashkenazic congregation in America. In the years of
its existence it has achieved fame as the wellspring of the
Conservative movement and the moving force in the founding
of the Jewish Theological Seminary of America. But more than
this, since 1825 Congregation B'nai Jeshurun has served as a
symbol of Judaism universal, a citadel of faith, learning,
and hope for all Jews.

liberal arts and sciences under Jewish auspices in America. It began as the first Jewish all-day school—Yeshivah-Etz-Chaim—on the Lower East Side of New York. In 1945 New York State granted Yeshivah university status.

There are five principal library collections at Yeshiva University. The historic main building of Yeshiva, erected in 1928 in upper Manhattan, is one of the outstanding examples of Byzantine architecture in Greater New York. Recently constructed was a seven-story residence hall and student center which has thirty-five modern class rooms and serves the seminary and colleges, graduate schools and institutes at the Main Center. It has three large lecture halls, conference rooms, faculty offices, a lounge, and a bookstore.

The Albert Einstein College of Medicine of Yeshiva University is located in the Borough of Bronx and is the first medical school established under Jewish auspices in America. It was founded in 1955. The college is the heart of a $100-million-dollar medical center that includes a $40-million-dollar hospital center constructed by the City of New York and a $45-million-dollar psychiatric hospital established by the State of New York.

Orthodox Jews in the city are organized in the Union of Orthodox Congregation and in various other rabbinical organizations such as the Rabbinical Council of America, the Misivta Torah Vadaath of Brooklyn, and the Mizrahi and Agudath movements in each of New York's five boroughs.

Conservative Judaism as a philosophy and a program received its great impetus under the leadership of Rabbi Doctor Sabato Morais, who helped organize the Jewish Theological Seminary in New York in 1886. The national prestige and character of its first two great presidents, Dr. Cyrus Adler and his successor in 1937, Dr. Louis Finkelstein, now emeritus has had much to do with the steady growth of the seminary and of Conservative Judaism.

The Jewish Theological Seminary, on Broadway and 122nd Street, contains the greatest collection of Judaica and Hebraica in the world. But the most interesting development of recent years has been the Jewish Theological Seminary's Jewish Museum at 1109 Fifth Avenue. Exhibitions here are devoted to the Yiddish theater, immigration, and every-day life in America, as well as to the fine arts where the work of Jewish painters, sculptors, and illustrators are displayed.

The Reconstructionist movement in New York took shape with the publication in 1934 of *Judaism as a Civilization*, by Dr. Mordecai M. Kaplan. The Jewish Reconstructionist Foundation was founded in 1940, but there has been no serious or actual attempt to organize Reconstructionist congregations en masse. The development remains primarily a "school of thought." For example, I know at least two Conservative rabbis who consider themselves adherents of Reconstructionism. And while there are some Reconstructionist congregations, it is hard to get any reliable statistics on the movement.

The student who reverently passes through these institutions to become an ordained rabbi, however, will find that learning is not as venerated among the Jews who form a congregation as it is within the seminary or the graduate school. The rabbi—the word means "teacher"—historically adjudicated Orthodox law. He was there to regulate the Jewish concept of holiness and make it workable.

His congregation today may never ask him for this wisdom. Where once Jews came to the rabbi to determine matters of profound spiritual and religious significance, now they will ask him on what days Purim will fall in 1972. They will plead with him to attend a circumcision. They will expect him to work closely with

The occasion of B'nai Jeshurun's 140th anniversary coincided with the fifteenth year of spiritual leadership of distinguished Rabbi William Berkowitz.

Rabbi William Berkowitz is the founder, director and moderator of the Institute of Adult Jewish Studies, which sponsors a nationally prominent lecture series, begun in 1951. His published books include *I Believe: The Faith of a Jew, Ten Vital Jewish Issues, Heritage and Hope: Dialogues in Judaism, Let Us Reason Together.*

129

the Hadassah on some events and to visit the sick and to provide an invocation, if asked, for the Chamber of Commerce luncheon. He is expected to lend comfort and advice to the parents of a teen-ager arrested for possessing marijuana and he is urged to talk to politicians about slum clearance, discrimination, and pollution and to speak out in the pulpit about the war in Vietnam.

But they do not need his instruction about worship, prayer, or faith. They do not want complaints about the poor attendance in the temple on Friday night nor do they think their children need more than two and a half hours a week of Hebrew School. The congregation will inform the rabbi that it is not necessary to be Jewish twenty-four hours a day, but they do insist he worry twenty-four hours a day about intermarriage, and when it occurs, which it does with increasing frequency, that he do something!

The rabbi will accept the fact no less than the minister and the priest that the laymen have taken over many of the prerogatives of the clergy. And the rabbi, if he wants to remain a rabbi, will make the best of it.

In their four-thousand year history the Jews have been assimilated a thousand times over. They have become for a time more Roman than the Romans, more German than the Germans, and at present, more middle-class American than middle-class America. They have remained Jews because they have the Law and sooner or later they will want again to obey it.

The Williamsburg section of Brooklyn is the Meah Shearim of the United States. The Meah Shearim area of Jerusalem is the home of the ultra-Orthodox Hasidic Jews: The Lubavicher Rabbi, the leader of the Hasidic fellowship, presides, however, in Williamsburg. Hasidism was founded by Baal Shem Tov in Lubevich, Poland, in the middle of the eighteenth century. The Baal Shem Tov taught his disciples by parables and upheld a pantheistic doctrine and communion with God through joyous worship. The present-day Lubavicher rabbi is Joel Teitelbaum whose seat of authority is at Williamsburg's Yetter Lev-D'Satmar, which has fifteen hundred members and serves over five thousand children in religious and Hebrew classes.

The last time I was in Williamsburg was about forty-five years ago, before the Hasidim came. In those days it was great fun to walk across the newly constructed Williamsburg Bridge spanning the East River. On the Brooklyn side, the Williamsburg sec-

The Jewish Museum was established by the Jewish Theological Seminary which was founded in 1886 to serve Conservative Judaism. Its first curator was the late Chief Rabbi Dr. Herman Hertz.

tion stood out with the beautiful brownstone residences of the rich.

Today as I walk these streets, I keep thinking of my mother, who was a pious woman. She worried about the kosher butchers on the Lower East Side. She thought they were careless about the strict kosher regulations. In present-day Williamsburg my mother would have been satisfied. Here the meat can't be simply kosher, it has to be *glat* kosher—kosher beyond the shadow of a doubt. Also, the butcher must be a Hasid himself; no one else is trusted. And each of the glat kosher butcher stores in Williamsburg carries the name of a sponsoring *rebbe* and of the rebbe's organization, with a printed notice that the profit goes to the religious school of that particular organization. In one shop window a notice says the profit goes toward the purchase of another bus for transportation of the school children.

There's another thing about present-day Williamsburg which would have pleased my mother. I once showed her a picture of a famous rabbi, Dr. Stephen S. Wise, and she thought I was teasing her; whoever heard of a great rabbi without a beard? She would have been perfectly satisfied in Williamsburg today. For here are the Hasidic men with the beards and *payess* (earlocks), wearing their long black coats and broad-brimmed hats; here are the little boys with side curls wearing *yarmulkahs* and the married women wearing wigs. Young married women and unmarried girls are virtually indistinguishable, with the exception that maidens dress more modestly than their married sisters. But both dress more modestly than girls outside the section. The girls wear no mini-skirts or slacks. Their clothing is standard, high-necked dresses with long sleeves to the wrist and black stockings. The boys and girls are segregated from each other at an early age and they do not mix in school or play.

On Thursday afternoon these Hasidim begin preparing for the Sabbath; the women, carrying their bundles of produce and fowl, fill the streets.

In a radius of forty square blocks, Williamsburg has forty-two synagogues of varying sizes, the majority of which are Hasidic. The neighborhood is dotted with stores selling wigs and turbans so that the women can keep their heads covered. There are at least thirty *mikvehs* (ritual baths) in the area. There is a hardware store that sells *Shabbes zeigers*, automatic devices used to operate the refrigerator and other electrical appliances by remote control on the Sabbath when no work may be done.

My guide on a recent tour through Williamsburg was the late Mr. George Swetnick. On every one of the streets of the district Hasidim stopped Mr. Swetnick to thank him for the new childrens' playground the city had just built. Mr. Swetnick was the Democratic boss of the district and an elected member of the New York City Council. When I asked him for a brief run-down on the politics of the district, he told me, "There are about forty thousand here—men, women, and children; my entire district includes about a quarter of a million people—Jews, Poles, and a growing population of Puerto Ricans."

A few blocks further on, talking to himself but loud enough for me to hear, this old professional politician sighed: "I've heard that my next opponent will be a Puerto Rican."

Only in America—and New York . . .

# CHAPTER 7

# The Earliest Beginnings

WHEN THE PORTUGESE conquered northern Brazil in 1654, they offered the Dutch colonists there the choice of staying and becoming loyal subjects of Portugal or of leaving the country within three months. Among the many colonists who chose the latter course were several hundred Jews, who a century earlier had fled the Inquisition in Spain and Portugal and who now wanted no part of their previous fellow countrymen.

Most of these early Jewish settlers in the New World returned to Europe and particularly to Holland, which was hospitable to many such outcasts. But a smaller group sailed for islands in the Caribbean. Oddly enough, a ship from Brazil, the *Valk*, bound for the Netherlands with twenty-three Jewish men, women, and children on board, brought the first Jewish immigrants to New York City. The small ship was captured by a Spanish pirate, then recaptured from the Spaniard by a French privateer, the *Saint Charles*. The French captain, Jacques de La Motthe, demanded 2,500 guilders of the group for passage to the nearest Dutch port of call, which was New Amsterdam.

In September of 1654 this tiny band of immigrants landed in the then-unimpressive village of New Amsterdam. Their reception was mixed. The French captain auctioned off the Jews' property as a means of raising more of the ransom money the refugees owed him. The Dutch burghers bought the goods, later returned them to their owners, and in some cases took the newcomers into their own homes. Still, many of the Jewish settlers

Homework involving the entire family: father, mother, children. It brought an extension of the sweatshop into the home.

camped out in the open and suffered through a severely cold and miserable first winter.

From twenty-three, the number of Jews in the city has grown to more than two million in 1970.

Next to the story of the English who landed at Jamestown and Plymouth Rock, the Jewish exodus from Europe to the United States is the greatest immigrant story ever told, and it is as romantic in its own way as the winning of the American West.

The immigrant enjoyed the fruits the pioneer bequeathed and now the third generation enjoys the fruits the immigrant bequeathed. Certainly the immigrant came from unfashionable places—from Romania, Poland, Lithuania—but I feel it is no overstatement to say the immigrant who squatted under dim lights for fourteen years sewing ladies' garments and went out on strike and came back to a workbench and a shorter work week underwent the same serious hardships and displayed the same spirit that the pioneer did.

For about a year and a half my family lived on Broome Street. Across from us was a saloon and a gambling house owned by Big Jack Zelig, who was later killed on a streetcar before he could testify against police Lieutenant Charles Becker, on trial for the murder of Herman Rosenthal.

In this tenement on Broome Street—the number was 295 if I'm not mistaken—there lived four families on each floor with a single toilet per floor. The families included mother, father, maybe some grandparents, anywhere from three to five children, and two or three boarders.

But that was only half of the story. The other half was that the tenement was also a factory; a whirling, churning factory where men, women, and children worked at sewing machines and pressing machines. These were the days before the cloakmakers' union became strong, before the International Ladies' Garment Workers' Union gained power.

In one of the rooms four men would sit, one or two women, a couple of young girls, ages anywhere from nine to fourteen, and perhaps an eleven-year-old boy working after school; and they were all working on knickerbockers or "knee pants," as everybody called them in the tenements and in the trade.

It was all piecework. The rate of pay a worker earned was based on the quality of the knee pants. The cheaper the grade of knee pants, the cheaper the rate of pay. The average was about seventy-five cents a dozen for the complete operation. This complete operation included everything from the cloth to the finished garment. This would leave a family of, say, five about fifteen dollars a week. Payment was at the rate of two cents a pair for the presser; thus the hot irons were kept on the stove in the heat of the summer (the season), so that the presser (usually the father, a grown son, or one of the boarders) always had an iron available. The children would handle piles of knee pants after the mother and the father got through with the sewing and pile them up for the finisher. The finisher, a young girl, received ten cents a dozen. These young girls (and often the wife) were all considered "learners," which enabled the contractor to pay them whatever wages he chose and also enabled everybody to circumvent whatever labor laws were on the books.

To a certain extent, this pernicious system was even advantageous to the worker. It supplied him with a source of immediate income on virtually the day after his arrival; and no matter how small the pay, he looked upon his employer as his benefactor. As his pay was often too small to support a large family even in the poorest imaginable style, it became necessary for his wife and children to join him in work, and the "benefactor" with his sweatshops, often a friend from the Old Country, provided them all with work. It was fortunate that this system extended only to a few "Jewish" industries and so affected but little the average

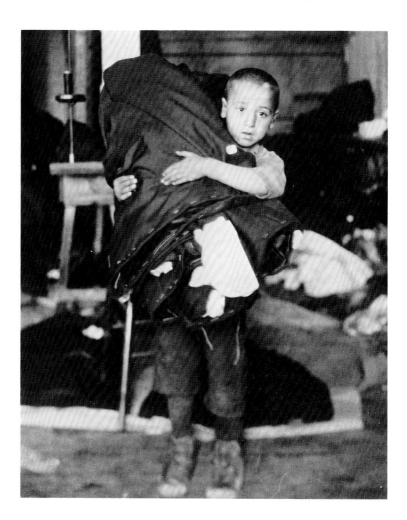

Whole families were involved in homework and the little boy pictured here was probably delivering the bundles of finished garments to the contractor. His salary would have been about twenty-five cents a week.

New York workingman involved in productive employment—or the opposition against the Jewish employers would have been strong and in a measure justified. The sweatshop, however, is not an exclusively Jewish institution; it has been, and remains, widespread. Italians to a large degree share it.

Nevertheless, the sweatshop, with its inevitable trinity of harmful consequences—low wages, long hours, and female and child labor—remained the essential economic problem of the Jewish population of New York City for the first three decades of this century. Of the horrors of the sweatshops so much has been written and spoken that scarcely an intelligent New Yorker can be found who is not to some degree aware of their evils. Private investigators as well as official committees have made thorough

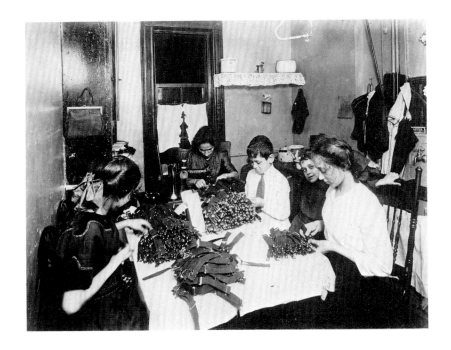

Homework.

studies of the institution. The peculiar conditions of the clothing industry, which made home work and the exploitation of ignorant immigrants so easy, facilitated the establishment of the system. The "green" immigrant who knew nothing of the conditions of the market was an easy prey to the sharks of his own or any other nationality. The subcontracting system, which meant working at home, was a fierce competitor to the legitimate factory. There weren't many laws defining working conditions, but there were some. All of them, however, excluded "learners," an innocent-sounding term which now contains in retrospect implications of awful exploitation.

The boarders paid two dollars and fifty cents a week for sleeping accommodations and breakfast, and everybody worked twelve hours a day, their goal to turn out from fifteen to twenty dozen pairs of knee pants. The ten-year-old would barely earn enough from a week's work to buy one pair of knee pants for himself.

And of course all this work was seasonal. Five months of the year the machines were silent, the knee-pants workers idle. Often in slack periods the father of the house carried his machine on his shoulder and went from factory to factory asking for a day's work. The average pay of the family often went as high as twenty-five dollars a week if they worked from six A.M. to eleven

Sweatshop scene in 1910. The employees worked ten hours a day, six days a week, for $12 a week. The industry was a jungle until the coming of the International Ladies' Garment Workers' Union which made life more bearable.

P.M. A few blocks farther north, on Stanton Street, were the tenements where the experienced tailors worked whole families making men's coats at an average of twenty-seven cents a coat. Each was delivered to the contractor with all operations complete except for buttons and buttonholes, which the contractor would let out elsewhere.

Many of these families wept when the industry became unionized in 1912 and 1914. They were afraid they would lose their livelihood. In such ways does poverty feed upon itself. Thus free enterprise in its purest state existed on the Lower East Side, among all the "foreigners" and principally among the Jews, who knew all there is to know about living in a competitive world.

The International Ladies' Garment Workers' Union (ILGWU) was founded in 1900, followed by the Cap Makers' Union in 1901, the Fur Workers' Union in 1904, and the Amalgamated Clothing Workers' Union (ACWU) in 1914. The mass strikes of 1909–14, known as the Great Revolt, and the 1911 Triangle Shirtwaist Factory fire, which took the lives of 145 boys and girls, were the turning points in the history of the Jewish labor movement. The

Great Revolt and the Triangle fire gave this movement an impetus which it never lost.

The first general strike in the needle trades began on November 22, 1909, when twenty thousand Jewish factory girls, makers of blouses and skirts, walked out on their jobs. Upper- and middle-class women joined the picket lines after mounted police tried routing the strikers. For the first time, uptown Gentile help came to the Lower East Side sweatshop workers. Christian clergymen and churchwomen from all over the city picketed with the shop girls.

The following year the entire garment industry was paralyzed by the city's biggest strike when sixty thousand cloakmakers put down their tools. Dismayed by the bitterness of the struggle between Jewish workers and Jewish employers, and by the use of Jewish thugs to assault strikers, the uptown Jewish community helped bring about a settlement. Louis Marshall and Jacob Schiff, with the aid of Louis D. Brandeis, who came down from Boston to serve as chairman of the mediation board that drafted "the protocol of peace," marked a milestone in the history of industrial relations. The settlement sounded the death knell of the sweatshop by abolishing piecework in the home and contractors' shops. It also gave the workers shorter hours, higher

The great strike of the shirtwaist makers in 1909. Above, the strikers are on the way to City Hall to make their protest.

139

Women picketing in front of a New York factory during ladies' tailors' strike.

wages, and decent working conditions, and set a precedent for peaceful resolution of labor conflicts in other industries by creating a permanent arbitration machinery.

But change did not come so quickly. Leon Stein, editor of the union paper *Justice,* described one tragic day in the life of a young girl working in one of the old-style sweatshops in his book, *The Triangle Fire.* Lucy Weintraub, nineteen years old, stands within the burning framework of a window on the ninth floor. She wears a wide-brimmed hat and her long dark hair flows free behind her. The flames reach out and she inches away. But one finger of flame touches the hem of her skirt and suddenly she's on fire. She takes the wide hat from her head and sails it out into the street. Carefully she takes the money out of her purse and tosses it to the crowd below. Then as the coins ring on the cobblestones, Lucy's body crashes down.

The Triangle Shirtwaist Factory fire occurred on March 25, 1911. Within twelve minutes 145 bodies lay lifeless on the sidewalk or in the loft. In the rear, where the fire escape had collapsed under the weight of escaping workers, dozens of employees were sprawled in gruesome tribute to the callous indifference that pervaded the garment industry of that era. A police-

What was left of the Triangle Shirtwaist Factory after the fire of 1911.

man on duty in the park saw the first puff of smoke, spurred his horse to the entrance, and ran up the steps of the factory. The building was on fire, although the flames could not be seen from the outside. Inside, the fabric, the machines and furniture, and the workers were being incinerated. But of more lasting import, going up in smoke at that same exact moment were the very idea and the institution of the sweatshop.

The hopes and dreams of thousands of young immigrants had come crashing down to earth during the sweatshop era; but ultimately out of the Triangle tragedy came safety legislation, the trade unions, and leaders like David Dubinsky and Louis Stulberg. The immigrants' dreams of justice and economic opportunity became real again.

The Jewish unions wielded important political influence in New York. As the backbone of the Socialist party, they elected Meyer London to the House of Representatives, seated several Socialists in the state legislature, and enabled Morris Hillquit to make a remarkable showing in the 1917 mayoralty election.

David Dubinsky and his aides, including his successor Louis Stulberg, built in the ILGWU a union which today has 450,000 members with millions of dollars in its reserves and welfare fund,

Louis Stulberg, who has taken over from David Dubinsky as president of the giant Internal Ladies' Garment Workers' Union. The union today has 363,000 members with millions of dollars in its reserve and welfare fund which provides pensions, college scholarships, homes for the aged, low-cost housing in the city, and vacation grounds in the country.

providing pensions, college scholarships, homes for the aged, low-cost housing in the city, and vacation grounds in the country.

The union's membership rolls during the last half century tell us much about the improving economic conditions of New York Jewry. There was a time when the garment workers were nearly all Jewish. But the children of the immigrants secured an education and went into the professions or into business in the general community. Today Jews of New York (and America) have the highest percentage of self-employed people of any group in the nation.

Eventually the Italians came into the garment shops and the union, followed by the Negroes and the Puerto Ricans. Surprisingly, the important change now is the growing number of white Anglo-Saxon women who are coming into the sewing shops of the industry. These are girls and women of families who have been moving into the city during the past ten years as the one-family farms are gradually abandoned.

But there has been little ethnic change on the "other side" of the collective bargaining table of this $4-billion-dollar industry that clothes the women of America. The six thousand or more sewing shops of the industry are mainly Jewish-owned.

Still, today when I see the home of a Southern cotton-mill worker with its car in the driveway and the electric washing machine on the porch, I think of the contribution the Jews of New York have made to the organized labor movement in America. I remember teachers asking a boy, "What does your father do?" And the boy often answering, "My father is a striker." When I was a boy growing up in the first two decades of this century, most of our fathers were "strikers."

In 1914 Samuel Gompers was sixty-four and Sidney Hillman was twenty-seven.

Sam was a cigarmaker like his father before him; his brand of trade-unionism was modeled on the trade organizations of mid-Victorian England. Today Sam is thought of as a member of "the old fashioned school"—the man of action, the labor organizer who led the cause from the time of the Haymarket Riot in 1886 through the years immediately following the Great Steel Strike of 1919. He was no man of learning, no intellectual or mystic. He always insisted that you couldn't run a union on the fuel of revolutionary hot air. Yet this English son of Dutch-Jewish stock was immersed in a steambath of theories, movements, and reform ideas that saturated the atmosphere of New York's Lower East Side.

Sam Gompers, the father of American trade-unionism. His creed was simple and positive: the acquisition of freedom through tenure in a job. Recognizing the weak hold of the labor cause in the public mind, Sam lectured widely and wrote books and pamphlets. The public sensed the man's obsession. In the end he failed to make a success of his international federation. But during the course of his campaigns, American labor entered the mainstream of middle-class America.

Hillman on the other hand was an intellectual, a political exile from the tsar, a former member of the Jewish underground labor movement, a recluse and continual reader, a product of

143

Talmudic Lithuania. In marked contrast to Sam Gompers, Hill-man was noted for his spirit of tact and sweet reasonableness.

When the Amalgamated Clothing Workers' Union was formed in 1914 (after they seceded from United Garment Workers), Hillman was made president. The ACWU was to become the prototype of the modern industrial union. Its newspapers were run off in seven languages; it inaugurated unemployment insurance programs and co-operative housing. In the five-man Labor Advisory Board for the National Recovery Administration, two came from the ACWU. In F.D.R.'s "kitchen cabinet" Hillman represented labor. For the first time, labor entered into a partnership with government. And it was Hillman's destiny to make America aware of labor's ability to function in various areas of modern, complex industrial society.

Contemporary sociologists have stated that "socially and ideologically the wage workers are more middle class than has heretofore been assumed. But this assumption always guided Gompers and Hillman.

Today the ACWU runs several banks, and has an insurance company to act as carrier for various welfare funds negotiated by the union. The ILGWU has made housing history with massive co-operative projects along the East River and in old Chelsea. It also is trustee for amounts running to several hundred million dollars, covering medical care, vacations, hospitalization, retirement, and severance pay for its members. The financial reports of these unions are carefully audited; investments are guided by investment counsellors. Not long ago David Dubinsky made money available to the Rockefellers for a housing project in Puerto Rico.

During recent years the spirit that spearheaded the early labor union movement has taken interesting new directions. The most rapidly expanding area of American trade-unionism today is its increasing involvement with government employees—e.g., the American Federation of Teachers, the American Federation of State, County, and Municipal Employees, the American Federation of Government Employees. Younger Jews, many of them children and grandchildren of activists from the early Jewish labor union movement, raised in liberal homes during the administrations of Roosevelt, Truman, and Kennedy, are now active in the new public employee unions. In the old days the Yiddish

Samuel Gompers, the father of the trade union movement in America, addressing a meeting of the shirtwaist makers in 1909. Their strike which followed lasted seven months. It was finally settled in a victory for the strikers.

Jacob S. Potofsky, general president of the Amalgamated Clothing Workers of America, participated in the Hart Shaffner & Marx strike in Chicago in 1910 which resulted in a signed agreement that brought the employees back to work. Clarence Darrow was the attorney for the union and Carl Sandburg reported the story for his Chicago newspaper, the *Day Book*. Sandburg said that the theme song of the strikers was a parody of the Salvation Army song "In the Sweet Bye and Bye"—"You'll Get Pie in the Sky When You Die."

145

language was virtually the trademark of the labor union movement. Today the white-collar union men speak straight English; but the old concerns for social involvement and reform are as important as ever.

In addition to Samuel Gompers and Sidney Hillman, Jacob Potofsky, David Dubinsky, Joseph Schlossberg, David Lasser, Rose Schneiderman, Lucy Lang, David Levitsky, and Herbert Benjamin were well-known Jewish labor leaders.

Notable among Jewish labor organizations of New York City are the Amalgamated Clothing Workers' Union, the International Ladies' Garment Workers' Union, the Cap and Millinery Workers' Union, and the Furriers' Union.

In New York City some four hundred thousand Jews hold union affiliations.

The Workman's Circle of New York is an organization of Jewish workers offering an extended program of mutual aid, with a zeal for fostering the Yiddish language and Yiddish culture.

In 1970 it was found that, in the manufacturing industries of New York City, 34.9 per cent of the workers were Jewish; in construction industries, 14.5 per cent; transportation, 13 per cent. In domestic and personal services, 21 per cent.

Almost every Jewish community in New York provides some kind of training or guidance and some place of vocational training.

The rabbis of New York have supported every movement—legislative or otherwise—to increase wages, to reduce hours of toil, and to render working conditions humane. The Central Conference of American Rabbis has from time to time given assistance, both financial and moral, to workers on strike.

# CHAPTER 8

# You Call This *Work?*
# (Compliments of
# Tom Sawyer)

ONE OF NEW YORK's great institutions, R. H. Macy's, accommodates every citizen in the city. The store, billed for years as "The World's Largest," employs some 1,400 clerks, many of whom are bilingual; as a group they speak forty-two languages, which is probably enough to take care of customers who want a bedspread or a pair of socks for their nephew. During the Christmas season, Macy's cash registers ring up $3 million on a single Saturday. Their policy of service, we can assume, has paid dividends.

And service is what you get at Macy's. Mail order departments try to satisfy customers who want "a dead horse for eel bait" or a special armchair that can be used for horizontal lovemaking. Shopping guides assist customers who are looking for such things as an elephant gun, a left-handed pair of scissors, rabbit-skin pajamas, or a crystal chandelier. You also get low prices. Macy's comparison-shoppers buy merchandise all over the city, and if they find an item for less than it is offered at Macy's, Macy's own price comes down the same day. Personal attention to customers is another store policy, in a city where such a courtesy is rare; recently when a newly wed couple complained that their bedroom furniture had not been delivered, Macy's sent a bed by special truck to the rescue.

Rowland Hussey Macy was a Quaker from Nantucket, a square-built man who had been schooled, like Herman Melville, in the whaling fleet. After two or three poor starts in Massachusetts, opening small shops which did not prosper, Macy opened a dry-goods store on Fourteenth Street and Sixth Avenue. The year was

R. H. Macy's, a New York tradition.

1858. One of his commercial weapons was using a healthy proportion of his profits for advertising, most of which he wrote himself. Another was the Nantucketer's sense of adventure; he experimented with different sales items; he branched out; soon he had what would soon become known as a "department store." During his first year Macy pulled in $90,000 in volume sales; by 1876, sales had risen to over one and a half million.

At Macy's death the store passed into the hands of two junior partners, Abiel La Forge and Robert Macy Valentine. La Forge died shortly thereafter, and Valentine brought into management a Macy relative and employee, Charles B. Webster. This gentleman, in turn brought in his brother-in-law, Jerome B. Wheeler. After a number of disagreements, Webster broke off with Wheeler and bought him and his stock out in 1887.

What has all this to do with the Jews of New York City?

Well, hang in there.

When Webster found himself standing alone in that huge store, with all that merchandise and all those customers, he went looking around for some new blood which might help him revitalize the whole operation. And that's what he found in the family of Lazarus Straus.

YOU CALL THIS WORK? (COMPLIMENTS OF TOM SAWYER)

Straus was a Jewish grain-merchant from Bavaria who came to America in 1848. With four sons he opened a little store in Talbotton, Georgia, supported the Confederate cause during the Civil War, and afterward moved to Philadelphia and then to New York where he started a wholesale chinaware importing firm known as L. Straus & Sons. The company had done business with Macy's since 1874; Straus leased departments in the store to sell china, glassware, and silver. Eventually the Strauses became partners with Webster and ultimately bought him out. From that day to this the Strauses have effectively managed the world's largest store.

Isidor Straus was sensitive, nervous, and a worrier. Nathan, his younger brother, was popular, enthusiastic, outgoing, and a natty dresser. Together they built Macy revenues from $5 million in 1888 to $10 million in 1902, which was incidentally, the year the store moved uptown to Thirty-fourth Street. During the succeeding decades of the new century, the Strauses expanded by buying interests in various stores in the Midwest and California, as well as opening branches of Macy's in many outlying areas of New York. In 1922 Macy stock was offered to the public, with the Straus family retaining control.

Isidor Straus gallantly went down with the *Titanic*, refusing to enter a lifeboat while women and children were still aboard the sinking ship. His sons Jesse and Percy had already assumed the management of the store. Their younger brother, Herbert, and the two sons of Nathan Straus also contributed to its many-faceted operation. Jesse and Percy ultimately bought out Nathan's interest, with Jesse assuming the top position for a while; finally the leadership descended on his oldest son, Jack. Various other members of the Straus family continue active in different departments and branches.

From its beginnings in the dream of a Nantucket whaler to its present status as the successful retailer to millions, R. H. Macy's is not only a part of the New York City scene, it is a part of the American story.

While we're discussing Macy's, let's not forget its prominent Herald Square neighbor, Gimbel's, Gimbel Brothers was founded

149

in 1842, in the then frontier town of Vincennes, Indiana, by Adam Gimbel, an immigrant peddler from Bavaria. He inaugurated the one-price policy in the area and advertised: "Fairness and Equality of All Patrons, whether they be Residents of the City, Plainsmen, Traders or Indians." The first of the modern Gimbel stores opened in Milwaukee in 1887. A Philadelphia store, since grown to many acres of space, was opened in 1894. New York was invaded in 1909. The Saks Company was absorbed by Gimbel's in 1923, Saks Fifth Avenue was opened the next year and the Kaufmann and Baer Company of Pittsburgh purchased in 1925. Under dynamic Bernard F. Gimbel, one of the founder's grandsons, who became president in 1927 and board chairman in 1953, the firm developed unusually forceful advertising and promotion. Expansion carried it into Chicago, Detroit, Beverly Hills, Miami Beach, San Francisco, and elsewhere. Bruce Alva Gimbel of the fourth generation succeeded his father as president. Gimbels had sales of $566,-336,000 in one year alone, in this case in the year ending April 30, 1966.

Nathan M. Ohrbach has a simple and very effective professional philosophy: "The housewife likes to feel that her favorite stores are not *selling* to her—they are *buying* for her. She is paying for a service. . . ." Today Ohrbach's in New York is famous for high style ladies wear at low cost, and its policy of "a business in millions, a profit in pennies," which is literally true of its operations, has made it one of the most successful retailing enterprises in the United States. From a small beginning on Fourteenth Street, Ohrbach's now sells in six stores in the New York and Los Angeles areas. Members of the garment industry plant dresses in Ohrbach's to see if they will sell in quantity. Ladies from all strata of society visit Ohrbach's to find bargains. Originality and imagination so distinguish Ohrbach's advertising that it has a permanent niche in New York folklore. In 1965 total sales of the entire Ohrbach's organization were estimated at almost $94 million.

Nathan Ohrbach came to America with his parents at the age of two, from Vienna, Austria. He grew up in Brooklyn with three brothers, opened small clothing shops in his twenties, and by 1923 had saved some money and spent eighteen of his thirty-eight years in retailing. With Max Wiesen, a dress manufacturer, Ohrbach opened a large retailing operation at the famous Fourteenth Street location, across from the already established S. Klein's, whose slogan was "On the Square." On Ohrbach's opening day in 1923,

Nathan M. Ohrbach, owner of the famous Ohrbach's department store and a powerful influence in the world of women's fashions.

Sam Klein came in for a look-see. "Such long counters!" he chuckled. "Such high ceilings!" Klein was amused. "It must be a joke. I'll give them just seven months." Klein was wrong. Ohrbach's was not only a success from the start, it was a near-riot. Customers on opening day overwhelmed the store clerks, bought up all the merchandise, overturned tables, and left a score of persons bruised and battered. Police were called in. Merchandise was rushed to the store to refurbish the bare tables and racks. This was to be a repeated ritual on "sale days" at Ohrbach's.

In 1954 Ohrbach's make the bold move of relocating on Thirty-fourth Street, thus coming into competition with Macy's and Gimbel's, not to mention the more exclusive department stores on lower Fifth Avenue. Ohrbach's not only made a go of it in the new location, they astounded their competitors. One hundred thousand customers crowded into their new store and spent half a million dollars on opening day. Macy's advertised: "If you live through this, you are ready for Macy's."

In the 1960s Nathan Ohrbach and his son Jerome merged interests in Ohrbach's with the Brenninkmeyer family, which had built a mercantile empire in many cities of Europe, with a home base in Holland. Nathan and Jerome then quietly slipped into the background, and the exact stock ownership in the company, as regards the Ohrbachs and the Brenninkmeyers, still remains unknown.

Meanwhile, on Thirty-fourth Street, the rush goes on. On sales days the manager opens the front doors and the ladies charge for the bargain tables like track men at the sound of the starting pistol. One story that has for years made the rounds of Ohrbach's clerks concerns a genteel and high-class lady who one day was caught in a crush around the glove table and was pushed into another lady customer. "Oh, I beg your pardon," said the high-class shopper. "I simply could not help myself." The other woman looked at her and muttered, "If you're so damned polite, why aren't you shopping at Altman's?"

Wedged between Times Square and Herald Square, and bordered by Seventh Avenue on the one side and Broadway on the other, but spilling over east and west, is the most temperamental one-tenth of a square mile in the world, otherwise known as the Garment District. Easily the most colorful part of the needle trade is the $4-billion-dollar-a-year women's clothing industry that has

David Schwartz, largest manufacturer in the garment industry (Jonathan Logan), operates fifty-six industries in New York, New Jersey, and the South.

its headquarters in this neighborhood. On Seventh Avenue the people who work at it, for it, and in it call it the "rag game."

Much of the success of this business depends upon fluctuating emotions in the American home. The wife looks in the closet one day and gets a deprived feeling. She turns to her husband and says, "Do you know, Sam, I haven't a thing to wear." That Saturday she comes home with a slight bulge in her shopping bag. "What's in the bag?" says Sam. "Oh, just a little nothing," she says.

Last year the American husband spent $10 billion dollars on these little nothings. But what the housewife calls a little nothing, the manufacturer calls a "rag." Rags are made everywhere, but more of them are made and sold in New York City than anywhere else in the world.

More than ten thousand firms are squashed into a few dozen office buildings between Thirty-fifth Street to the south and Forty-second Street to the north. Nowadays a good deal of the actual sewing is done in places as far away as Puerto Rico and South Carolina. But a buyer still wants to find the goods all in one place.

The garment industry resembles India with its caste system. The people on Seventh Avenue tend to look down their noses at the folks on Broadway. Even the buildings have caste. Take this adjoining pair—530 and 559 Seventh. The biggest names in American design work here. Most of the garments mapped out in these two buildings wholesale for fifty to five hundred dollars each. Quite a business. Status is just as important on Seventh Avenue as it is on Park.

On Seventh, rags are known as "the collection."

Over on Broadway, the home of the low and medium price dress houses, the rags are more modestly described as "the line."

To be somebody in Broadway's pecking order, a manufacturer must have space to show his line either at 1400 Broadway or across the street in 1407. Inside both buildings are the headquarters for most of the nation's biggest dress companies. A typical dress company here will have a sample room in the back. That's where the new line is designed. And a showroom in the front. That's where the line is displayed to the buyers. Outside, the sidewalks are jammed from morning till night with trucks bringing in dress samples or loading fabric to take to the out-of-town factories.

The streets are also crowded with pipe racks, push trucks and wheel barrows, and, when all else is missing, with the shoulders of the boys who shunt the garments from one building to another, at times displaying as much temper or temperament as their bosses.

Squeezed into the surrounding side streets are the service trades that supply the garment center—trimming and button stores and sewing machine outlets.

An interesting phenomenon of the trade is the way in which everyone can be identified in the garment center. Remember aircraft recognition? Well, there is a system just as precise known as "Garment District recognition."

For example, no salesman there would be caught dead in a business suit. This is one of the big differences between Seventh and Madison Avenues. The Garment Center insists on non-conformity in dress as in other matters and may be the last refuge of individualism in New York. Then there are the models rushing into the buildings, easily recognizable because they are always in a hurry between assignments. And you can always spot a buyer; he favors either a big manila envelope or a leather portfolio; inside are his merchandising schedules and order forms. The harassed-looking young girl is probably an assistant buyer, a fancy title for a job that consists primarily of chasing the showroom salesmen who promised early delivery.

"What's new?" the man wants to know. "Nice material! Who's the resource [where did it come from]?" In the garment business these are routine and inevitable questions. Because the industry is seasonal, because tastes and fashions change so rapidly, the answer to the question "What's new?" is one of the basic pieces of information needed for survival.

In the warm summer months in New York City there's no place like Seventh Avenue for a nice schmooze. At lunch hour the workers pour out of the showrooms and the workrooms for a little conversation. It may concern the boss. It may be about the general state of business. In any case, this is one of the more pleasant aspects of the trade, its easy informality. When the boss closes a deal, to take another example, he's likely to shake hands on it right out in the open at lunchtime. You don't catch a garment manufacturer hiring a hotel room for such an occasion.

Another point on the district's informality: the sidewalk's a great place to find out what the competition is up to. Is Meyer cutting velvet? Will hemlines be lower? Do you think we're going to have a cold winter? Or a warm fall? In the rag game, time is measured by the season. Five seasons make a garment district year—spring, summer, fall, winter, and slack.

Timing is the key to success (or failure) in the rag business. There's a cat-and-mouse game always played between the buyers and the manufacturers. The dressmaker wants to wait as long as possible before actually cutting material. Until he has the buyer's order he isn't gambling. The buyer on the other hand likes to think it over. Meanwhile with no orders coming in, the manufacturer may have to borrow money to get by. Once the order does come in, the boss gives the word to buy the fabric and start cutting. Wedding dresses, for example, wholesale at about forty dollars each, and the cutter cuts them one hundred and fifty at a time.

The competition on Seventh Avenue is murder, with every season a frantic gamble. And competition has kept the garment business highly fragmented. George Maurer's wedding dress business and Abe Fortgang's midtown blouse factory are typical of the specialization in New York's garment center. Fewer than two out of ten companies do better than $5 million in sales a year. Most do much less. Fabric is the manufacturer's biggest expense. Before he buys he wants to make sure it's going to be a hit. Since this is not possible, all he can do is hope his guess is right. His next biggest expense is labor. Someone once said it takes three hundred and sixty different steps to make a dress. And then the customer says, "I don't like it."

A dress begins with a sketch and proceeds to a sample. I imagine this is what Detroit would call a "prototype." Then a pattern-maker takes over. His is highly skilled work. Next the pattern is "marked up." At this point a manufacturer can lose his shirt. The point of this operation is to get as many sections of a garment out of the one bolt of cloth as possible. Nine times out of ten the man that does the marking is also the cutter. Cutters are the aristocrats of the garment industry. A good cutter earns several hundred dollars a week. At the same time he can usually save his boss several hundred a week in fabric with his skill.

Men seem to have the monopoly on the cutting, but women make up the larger proportion of the garment industry's employees. No matter what their job, as long as they're at a sewing machine they're called "operators" and are paid on a piecework basis. That way the boss gets more work done and they get a bigger paycheck.

More brassieres are made in New York than anywhere else in the world, which is one reason why the braless look originated in the mind of a Gotham columnist. As in the case of dressmaking, dozens of hand operations are involved in the manufacture of a good brassiere—something like forty operations required before it can be shipped to the lingerie counter. Then some guy unhooks it all deftly in a matter of seconds.

Historians of this uplifting area of American history generally credit the idea of mass-produced brassieres to a remarkable woman—a Mrs. Rosenthal. At seventy-nine she's still running the Maidenform Brassiere Company, which utilizes special machines that took years to develop. When visiting Russian politicos toured Mrs. Rosenthal's plant, they asked the manager if they could have a book describing the brassiere-making machines. Mrs. Rosenthal presented them with her latest catalogue. Strange ammunition is sometimes called for in the Cold War. The Russians went home happy, with something wondrous to show their comrades.

Thomas Jefferson put political freedom into the Declaration of Independence. And Nathan Komotow, a Jewish immigrant from Eastern Europe, helped put democracy into practice. Komotow invented a knife that cut through forty thicknesses of cloth at once. Editors can now wear the same suit as bank presidents. Before Komotow, it was homemade breeches for everybody except the bank presidents. The mail-order catalogue for 1908 indicates that the big sellers for men were overalls and pants. But Komotow's invention meant that a tailor could cut forty vests in five minutes, and no longer could you distinguish at sight a taxi driver from the owner of the cotton mill.

As the garment industry expands and its operations become increasingly complex, automation will no doubt play a larger and larger role in it. At present, it is semi-automated. One girl now tends five machines. Meanwhile the four other girls have been released to perform other jobs in the same factory, better paid ones at that. But eventually automation will be a serious problem for the members of the ILGWU.

ILGWU—the marvelous International Ladies' Garment Workers' Union. In the old days most garment workers lived on the Lower East Side, in the ghetto. One of the first things the ILGWU did when it acquired surplus funds was to invest in the aforementioned real estate for its members. And this union has always been concerned with the health and well-being of its constituents, long ago facing the realization that chicken soup can not cure all ills. Hence the ILGWU built health centers. The union is like the New York Police Department, in the sense that it is broken up into different precincts.

The boss in a shop has started a new style, and the girls who do the piecework want two-fifty for installing the zipper. The boss stands pat at two dollars. In comes the union adjuster. "You want to save money?" he says to the boss. "You want to compete? Compete on styling. Compete on material. Compete on anything, but not on labor. If there's work in the garment, it must be paid for." In the end both sides will settle, as always. The boss will concede that he has the best girls in the entire trade, and the girls will contend that they have the most generous boss. And the union . . . the union keeps the peace.

Four times a year some eight thousand buyers come into the city from all over the country. The buying offices (which act as agent for each of the big retail stores) fill the buyer in on the eternal question, "What's new?" Seventh Avenue does the sewing and selling, Madison Avenue does the shouting, Main Street consumes. The fashion magazines have, by the time of the buyers' visit, stirred up an unprecedented demand for this season's or even next season's model. Eleanor Lambert, one of the key buyers, is the highest paid woman in the fashion business.

Most dress showrooms are like bull rings. The salesman is the matador, the buyer is the bull. There are always spectators to the operation, waiting for the moment of truth. All that is lacking is the little brass band and Ernest Hemingway taking notes.

Every dress has to be sold three times: once to the buyer, once to the lady in the shop, and then again to the husband. If he disapproves, back it goes to the shop.

Detroit invented the mass-produced car. New York gave the world the mass-produced dress. But the one-of-a-kind item is still available for those who can afford Bergdorf Goodman. The prices start at eight hundred dollars. Down on Thirty-fourth Street the selection process is a bit harder, but the price tag a good deal easier. High fashion garments still have their place, but something had to give somewhere and today merchandisers have provided a customer break-through in what is known as the line-for-line copy. The New York buyer goes to a Paris fashion show and brings back new items, which are then torn apart and copied stitch for stitch.

Jonathan Logan is the giant of the women's wear business. It makes dresses not by the dozen, but by the thousands. And this enterprise was built up by one man—David Schwartz—who is still in charge of it all. He has bought up company after company, until he now controls the biggest dress empire in the city. In the process he has earned a reputation for being a tough man to deal with.

Another great name on Seventh Avenue is Pauline Trigère, who came here from France on a visit and decided to stay. Trigère's dresses start at about two hundred dollars, with nearly an unlimited ceiling. Her garments are made almost entirely by hand, one at a time; sewing machines are used sparingly, as salt in a gourmet's dinner. Trigère works from a model. Less than 2 per cent of each garment is machine-sewn. An embroidered evening gown takes hundreds of hours of hand work. One such gown sells for $3,500 in the shop.

At the average-priced level of the garment industry, there is word that the big companies are gradually gaining control and might eventually force the little man out. There are also indications that manufacturers have been leaving New York at an accelerated pace since World War II. They are going to Arkansas, the Carolinas, and other southern states, and to Puerto Rico— where they will enjoy tax concessions, cheaper labor, and non-union wages. Perhaps this exodus will continue. The ILGWU keeps after those factories running away to escape the union. They have representatives checking into these businesses who often use subterfuge to disguise their factories. In one instance in Alabama, the factory is called "Balance Agriculture with Industry Inc." It manufactures brassieres.

But the excitement, the designing, the sales, and the chutzpa will remain on Seventh Avenue in New York City. This is one business no computer, no tax concessions, no automation will ever replace. For the basis of the rag game has always been and will always be *individual imagination.*

Abel Green is five feet six and nattily dressed; he sits in *Variety* offices at a big desk elevated a few feet above the level of the rest of that floor and looks out through a larger-than-usual plate glass window at the auto and pedestrian traffic on West Forty-sixth Street.

"There is no ethnic frontier in show biz," Abel says unhesitatingly. One gets the unmistakable impression that Abel has been writing sharp and to-the-point stories for this famous show-business newspaper for so many years now that headlines and lead-paragraphs enter naturally into his conversation.

"Talent is talent is talent," he goes on. "Show biz doesn't care if you're Ethel Waters, Bojangles Robinson, Fanny Brice, or Randolph Scott. All show biz wants to know is can you sing, dance, recite a monologue, or act in a Western."

Abel Green ought to know. He has been writing reviews and features for *Variety* since 1918 and has been editor since 1933. During that time he has observed at close range the entertainment world as it flowered in vaudeville, the Broadway stage, and off-Broadway as well; night-club acts, radio, movies, and TV. Abel has written countless reviews and features for *Variety*, which

Abel Green, editor of *Variety.*

is sometimes called the "Bible of Show Business." He has popularized a short-hand slang show-biz dialect; when Abel writes LIZ BOMBS IN MOTOR TOWN, he means the new Elizabeth Taylor film has not attracted large audiences in Detroit. Such talk has not only made its contribution to colloquial American, but has attracted the interest of such readers as Francis Cardinal Spellman and George Bernard Shaw, who were *Variety* subscribers.

"New York might be the greatest Jewish city in the world," says Abel, "but it's also the greatest Italian city in the world, and probably the greatest Irish city in the world. For every Barbra Streisand there's a Lucille Ball. Pat Cooper is an Italian comedian who performs at Jewish rallies in Madison Square Garden; and Myron Cohen is a Jewish comedian who performed at Italian rallies in Madison Square Garden."

The telephone rings and Abel Green talks headlines into the mouthpiece for a few minutes, meanwhile making notes and editing phrases posted on various clip boards stationed in strategic spots on his big, cluttered desk.

"Show-biz management is largely in the hands of Jews, and the Frohmans and Belascos made an indelible contribution. Vaudeville comics even contributed Jewish words and phrases to the English language. 'What's your shtick?'—you hear it every day. But today we have Negro and Puerto Rican talent, Protestant talent, Catholic talent, all kinds of talent. That's the only thing that counts. In TV talk shows, you had five big names, and only one of them Jewish. He simply had less talent for that kind of thing."

The telephone rings again, and a copy writer drops something on Abel's desk.

"The Borscht Circuit? Sure. It was a cradle for playwrights, actors, comedians—Dore Schary, Red Buttons, Danny Kaye, Sid Caesar, Phil Silvers—but the Borscht Circuit is no more. Today it's a misnomer. You can't get borscht up there anymore, unless you order champagne and caviar on the side. Just like Tin Pan Alley. There's no such thing nowadays. The music producers have offices in skyscrapers made of glass and steel."

Abel picks up a book entitled *Famous Modern Newspaper Writers*, which contains chapters on James Reston, Art Buchwald, Heywood Broun, and Ernie Pyle. One of the chapters is devoted to Abel Green. "Here," he says. "If you want more information, read this." And as you are leaving, he says, "Speaking of the

Borscht Circuit, that's where Eddie Fisher got his start. You know, Eddie Fisher, the two-time loser. He first lost Debbie Reynolds, then he lost Elizabeth Taylor. *I should* be such a loser!"

It says in the book that Abel Green was born in 1900.

Abel Green is seventy-two?

The effects of American Jews clustering in the city led to their domination of show business and some branches of communications, as well as the garment industry, jewelry, and some of the traditional trades. In addition, publishing has not only been enriched but to a considerable extent shaped and reshaped by New York Jews. By Bennett Cerf, Alfred A. Knopf, Thomas Guinzburg, Dick Simon, and Max Schuster—all men who founded interesting book publishing houses fully as significant as the WASP operations at Scribner's, Doubleday, and, in the past, Macmillan.

The late David Sarnoff, was honorary chairman of the Radio Corporation of America and a pioneer in communications. He anticipated the radio and television and space travel. "I happened to be born about the time radio was born," Sarnoff once said, "and I happened to have gone along with it."

The young Jewish immigrant's first association with radio came on the night of April 14, 1912, as he flashed to the world the news of the sinking of the *Titanic*. He was a founder of the National Broadcasting Company in 1926. Sarnoff was the guiding spirit of the corporation that helped change America's listening and looking habits.

161

One of the most distinguished financial firms in the United States recently celebrated its hundredth anniversary. Kuhn, Loeb & Co., investment specialists, has served as financial adviser to such giants as Bethlehem Steel, Eastern Airlines, Westinghouse, and Western Union. K-L, as it is sometimes called, has clients in Tasmania, Sweden, Mexico, and Israel—to cite only a few of its overseas connections. At home it has managed underwriting groups that have sold billions of dollars in securities in the last decade alone.

The roots of this Jewish-American enterprise go back to Cincinnati to a time several years before the Civil War. There, Solomon Loeb, an immigrant to the United States from Germany, joined his distant relative Abraham Kuhn to become co-manager of a dry-goods business. The firm prospered to such an extent that eventually the two kinsmen, who by this time had also become brothers-in-law, accumulated $500,000 in capital and set out for New York to open an office "for the transaction of a general banking and commission business."

In 1875 Jacob Schiff, a twenty-eight-year-old immigrant from Frankfurt, was admitted to the partnership. He directed the company for the next forty-five years. Otto Kahn, the Maecenas of American arts, joined the firm in the 1890s. Schiff and Kahn struggled mightily in a series of encounters against James J. Hill and J. P. Morgan for control of the Northern Pacific Railroad. Schiff and Kahn won.

Another K-L partner who played a leading role in American financial history was Paul M. Warburg, one of the founders of the Federal Reserve System. Today the firm is headed by John Schiff and Frederick Warburg, plus an operating committee of six other partners.

Other Jewish banking firms in Wall Street included Ladenburg Thalman, & Company, Goldman Sachs, Lehman Brothers, Speyer & Company, and Hallgarten & Company. In addition, in 1970 there were 109 Jewish members of the New York Stock Exchange.

Jewish refugees from Antwerp who moved their businesses to New York in the wake of Hitler's conquests have established the most amazing diamond market in the world.

The Diamond Center runs from the lower Forties to the lower Fifties in the heart of what used to be known as the Great White Way—Broadway. Headquarters for this industry is West 47th Street between Fifth and Sixth Avenues.

Jacob H. Schiff, banker and philanthropist, was for many years the
Number One Republican of New York State.

Mr. Schiff was a descendant of a family known to have settled in
Frankfurt as early as 1370. In 1865, at the age of eighteen, he emigrated to
the United States where he became one of the leading figures of the
country. In 1875 he married Therese Loeb, daughter of Solomon Loeb,
head of the banking house of Kuhn, Loeb & Company. Schiff joined the
firm and displayed such acumen in banking affairs that he was made
head of the firm in 1885 when Loeb retired.

By the time he was fifty years old he had acquired the reputation
throughout the country as one of the greatest financiers among New York
bankers. Schiff's firm was also engaged in underwriting loans to foreign
governments. His outstanding achievement in international finance was the
floating of a $200 million bond issue for the Japanese government at the
time of the Russo-Japanese War 1904–5. Because he viewed the Czarist
regime as the enemy of all mankind on account of its oppression of Jews,
Schiff welcomed this opportunity to aid Japan.

Schiff's contribution to the development of American industry alone made
him an outstanding figure in American economic history. It is, however,
his philanthropic activities that entitle him to a leading place in the
American roll of honor and that have left a more permanent impress upon
the development of the United States. There was scarcely a good work
of public import of any description which Schiff did not encourage with
his moral and material support. These public activities were inspired by his
affection for his adopted country, an affection which was combined with
religious reverence. He joined at various times in memorial projects like
those of the Hudson-Fulton Celebration in 1909, the Washington Manor
House Fund, the Alexander Hamilton Association, the erection of a statue
of General William Tecumseh Sherman, and numerous others.

His granddaughter, Dorothy Schiff is publisher of the ultra-liberal
New York *Post*.

163

Shop windows filled with diamonds whose prices range from
$50 to $20,000 line both sides of the street which teems with uniformed policemen, private detectives, customers, buyers and cutters, polishers and setters. Booths line the entire ground floor of
each of the buildings, populated by dealers, appraisers, salesmen.
Above these booths, on each succeeding floor of each skyscraper
are the offices of a total of nearly four hundred diamond-cutting
firms, equipment suppliers, and diamond brokers.

The entire diamond business runs on credit and memoranda.
A nod of the head, a handshake, buyer and seller each repeating
*mazel 'n brocha*—a benediction for good luck—are enough to seal
a $100,000 deal in uncut stones. On any given day, there is liter-
ally over a billion dollars worth of diamonds along this street,
mostly in the pocket wallets of the individual buyers and sellers
who attach their wallets to an iron chain which in turn attaches
to a leather belt wrapped around the body.

Rarely is there a disagreement or a mistake in this business.
Many of these men belong to the Diamond Dealers Club of
America, whose charter demands that no member ever initiate
legal proceedings against another. When there is a disagreement,
the Diamond Dealers Club sets up an arbitration board whose
findings bind both parties. Its word is law and a member who

August Belmont, famous banker, the
American Rothschild.

Belmont's political influence was
impressive. From 1860 to 1884 he was
Democratic national committeeman.
Widely known as a patron of the
arts, he possessed one of the finest
collections of paintings in New York.
Owner of one of the finest racing
stables in the country, he was for
many years president of the American
Jockey Club and accomplished many
reforms in thoroughbred racing.

His wife shown in the photograph
above was the daughter of Commodore
Matthew Perry.

The New York
Diamond Dealers
Club. A handshake,
a *mazel 'n brocha,*
and a $100,000 deal
in uncut diamonds is
sealed.

breaches that law is drummed out of the industry—and almost immediately the word reaches London, Antwerp, Milan, Buenos Aires, Tel Aviv, and Johannesburg.

The Diamond Dealers Club controls the industry and really resembles a guild more than a club. Its membership is almost totally Jewish. Jack Sigmon, the president of the club, told me with a sad sigh, "We used to have four Gentiles as members, but one died last year; now there are only three." A significant number of hasidim are among the dealers; many others are the technicians. One of the hasidim dealers will pause momentarily in a crowded street doorway, open his black wallet and from it extract a small square of tissue paper, inside of which may be precious gems worth many thousands of dollars. He passes it over to a buyer, utters the "mazel 'n brocha," and then proceeds on his way to another doorway—a man from the Middle Ages, perfectly adept in the twentieth century.

Many more of the hasidim are polishers, setters, and cutters. At seven A.M. every morning most of the hasidim arrive in Manhattan in buses which have transported them over forty miles from their ultra-orthodox enclave at New Square, New York. For these pious Jews have created literally a Jewish *shtetl* in Rockland

165

The author and one of the directors of the directors of the Diamond Center of America discussing a point.

County in upstate New York. New Square is entirely new and entirely hasidic. Its women who also work in the diamond trade travel in a segregated section of the bus which always carries the Torah and the Eternal Light which shines on the Torah for the morning and evening services.

Each of the many organizations on Forty-seventh Street has a central room with lockers, tables, telephones, kosher cafeterias, bullet-proof windows, and burglar-alarm studded walls. Above the Diamond Dealers Club headquarters is a small synagogue where the dealers can retire for the afternoon *mincha* service.

At night the street is barren, the windows stripped of stone and ring. And all over the city and suburbs, there are hundreds of diamond dealers worrying, "Did I close that safe? Did I pull it tight?" Invariably they did, but one of the dealers told me, "We never stop worrying. Never."

Shlomo W., seventy-six years old and semiretired, has a unique occupation: he gives away money. Situated in a modest brownstone walk-up, Shlomo returns home from a daily trip to the bank with sums varying from fourteen to thirty-six hundred dollars. The exact amount is an important part of Shlomo's routine. He will rise in the morning, have breakfast (oatmeal with cream and sugar), read the paper, and then tackle the question: how much money shall I give away today? He deliberates, muses upon this question sometimes for as long as thirty minutes. Then he makes up his mind, and there is no going back on the decision. If Shlomo says, today I'll give away $850 (and often he hits upon just such an unpredictable sum), then he demands of himself that he give away exactly so much and no more. If he runs out of cash early, Shlomo has a strict policy which forbids a return to the bank after the first stop in the morning. If he finds that he still has funds left, come six in the evening, then he simply walks along the streets until he finds himself in an unfamiliar neighborhood (where he is not known) and selects a lounger or a street kid as the recipient of the day's balance.

Most of the benefactors of Shlomo's generosity are relatives, friends of relatives, relatives of friends, and relatives of relatives. Only rarely does Shlomo give money to absolute strangers; and these occasions occur with the unused surplus at a given day's end.

His procedure is very simple. The relative, or the friend of the relative, or the relative of the friend, or the relative of the relative is given Shlomo's address and a time of day printed on an ordinary bit of paper. The recipient must be at Shlomo's flat at exactly the prescribed hour; he knocks, is admitted, and Shlomo asks him, "How much?" Ordinarily the recipient states a sum and gets his money without further fuss. Sometimes, however, the amount stated will strike Shlomo as exorbitant, and then the haggling begins. "Why do you need that much?" "But, uncle, it's for my medicine . . ." Or perhaps: "But, brother-in-law, your sister wears out so many dresses, she is now wearing shmattes only, I swear . . ."

Sometimes such discussions go on for hours. Eventually there is a settlement, and the two part friends until the next time. Usually on such days a backlog of recipients piles up outside Shlomo's door, down the steps, and out into the street. But no matter. Shlomo concludes the rest of the day's business hurriedly, without interruptions. One of Shlomo's grandnephews has kept careful records and says that haggling occurs on an average of three times a month. One day last year, however, Shlomo haggled all day and threw the average off for the next two and a half years. There were traffic jams for blocks.

The hardest day he ever put in, says Shlomo, was oddly enough not the thirty-six-hundred-dollar day, which went very smoothly, but a day in 1962 when he took out eleven hundred dollars and

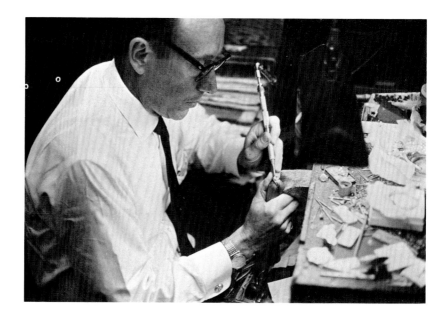

A diamond cutter in the Diamond Exchange in New York.

no one showed up, the entire circle of friends, relatives, etc., having been stricken by flu the day before and now confined to bed by doctors' orders. By noon that day Shlomo began to worry. By two o'clock he was in a panic. He called dozens of people on the telephone and urged them to come over, resorting even to picking numbers out of the directory at random. Then he sat back to wait. But no one came. Shlomo ran out into the streets, pressing twenty-dollar bills into the hands of little old ladies, throwing sawbucks at cops, tipping the cigar lady fifty dollars.

"Whew!" exclaimed Shlomo, adding several loud curses. "What a way to make a living!"

Shlomo acquired his considerable fortune by wisely investing the income, plus the insurance payments, from two former wives, both now deceased. He has been eating up capital for some time now but shows no sign that he is worried about running out. "What the hell," he says with a philosophic shrug of the shoulders. "It's just a job, like any other."

# CHAPTER 9

# "All These Are Gates
# of Our Lord"

PETER STUYVESANT of New Amsterdam wanted the twenty-three Jews from Brazil to get back on the ship from which they had just disembarked. He wanted to bar these Jews not so much because he despised their beliefs, but because if he set a precedent by admitting Jews, he would have to admit "Papists," Lutherans, and "unwanted immigrants," as he called Quakers.

The Jews petitioned the Dutch West India Company which rescinded Stuyvesant's proscription. The directors of the company noted that many Jews in Holland owned shares in the enterprise and that Jews had suffered in the war with Portugal, and they went on to instruct Stuyvesant that he must not "force people's conscience but allow everyone to have his own belief as long as he behaves quietly and legally. The poor among these Jews shall not become a burden to the Company or to the community, but be supported by their own nation."

Jews are conscious of life's difficulties. The important fact about American Jews is that almost as soon as they got settled here they proceeded to do something about the difficulties—to give help and assistance to other Jews who suffered from a wide variety of problems and hardships. They offered money, food and shelter, information and advice, care and consolation, medical attention, and other services. In providing charity they fulfilled one of the strongest traditions in Judaism—another instance of the Jews' preserving the principles and practice of their religious ethics. Of course, needy Jews had outside help too. In the early decades of the twentieth century, as I've mentioned, the settlement houses did noble work to benefit the immigrants; so did Tammany, in its way. But the Jewish tradition of self-help was a present from the earliest days of America. Jewish labor organizations, legal bodies, professional societies, philanthropic and loan agencies, the Jewish press—all these joined in the continuing struggle to assist the needy, the ignorant, the destitute newcomer and old-timer alike. This tradition has had a steady development in America; the organizations and agencies have proliferated until today they range from highly specialized services for the blind, the deaf, the aged, and the infirm, to help for erring teen-agers, unwed mothers, newly arrived immigrants, and asthmatic children—to offer only a small sampling.

At the same time such organizations, from the beginning, did more than benefit indigent Jews. By adopting a principle of "let no man or woman become a burden on the city," they created an atmosphere of concern that served as an inspiration to other ethnic groups in the city, and sometimes served as an embarrassment to those who were doing nothing. William Travers Jerome, district attorney of New York in 1901–9 and a first cousin of Lady Randolph Churchill, once observed in a campaign speech to an audience of rich, fellow Episcopalians: "My friends, you are one of my own class. I was born and bred with you. But I want to say to you that you are of no use to this city. I feel bitterly against you because of your heartlessness. Morally you are as bad as the people I am fighting in the lowliest dive. Every dollar you have laid by, every step you have climbed in the social scale, has laid upon you an obligation of civil leadership and you have failed. Do you think I want your votes? Take them to the political bosses who run this city. The only civic and welfare work being done in this city is being done by Irish charities and Russian Jews."

The Jewish welfare organizations faced a subtler problem than appeared on the surface—the attitude of many immigrants toward accepting charity. One of the few lasting impressions I carry with me from the old days on the Lower East Side is my mother's absolute aversion to charity of any kind. I suspect this was based on fear, the fear of becoming a welfare case, dependent upon the generosity of complete strangers in an unfamiliar land. Thus the fraternal organizations and charitable agencies of the time always spoke in terms of "benefits" in order to allay such fear and circumvent resistance. It was a good system; the idea of "benefit" displaced the feeling of helplessness from accident or sickness or unemployment; it emphasized the positive. No welfare worker said, "On account of the death of your husband, or the days missed because of illness . . ." Instead, she spoke of the "benefits" that were due, and she let it go at that. I firmly believe that in cases such as these the choice of words is all-important in influencing Fate. The Evil Eye cannot operate in the atmosphere created by the sound of the word "benefit."

JASA—the Jewish Association for Services for the Aged—handles two thousand cases every month. It sends out social workers into underprivileged neighborhoods to set up social clubs and recreation headquarters; they arrange for home care, housekeeping, medical and psychiatric aid; they visit the shut-ins, bring people together, and provide relief funds for emergency situa-

Scene of the first Seder night, April 30, 1970, co-sponsored by the Jewish Association for Services for the Aged and the Jewish community of Bensonhurst.

JASA is a new organization, created by the Federation of Jewish Philanthropies of New York specially to help meet the problem of the approximately 300,000 Jewish residents in New York City who are sixty-five years of age or over.

The Jewish Home and Hospital for Aged. One of many benevolent Societies that serve the interests and needs of Jewish Americans. The children are from PS122 in the Bronx.

tions. JASA has discovered that many Jewish aged are eligible for welfare, but do not know it. They help these people apply for public assistance; often they find that an older citizen has a small savings account of a few thousand dollars which he will not touch; he has to be prodded to spend some of it, in order to become eligible for welfare allotments. JASA is funded by the Federation of Jewish Charities and is staffed by many volunteer workers. Directors of the program agree that the problems of the aged are of epidemic proportions; there are not enough beds to go around in the city's nursing homes; there is insufficient housing that the old people can afford; there are not enough social workers to visit the homes of the desperate and the abandoned.

"I drove my own car for years," says Jake Aronstein, "until the thing started giving me so much trouble. I had it fixed a hundred times, and I prayed over it too. But I finally decided that God is not a mechanic, and now I do without it. One thing though"— and he drops his banter—"I miss the car, just as I miss the old days. Oh, I haven't got it so bad. I have found that once you start telling everyone about your problems, pretty soon you have nothing else to talk about. But the truth is, I don't have any friends any more, not really. Oh, there's a few people around, but mostly they want to use me for one thing or another. Yes, that's what I really feel the lack of, a good friend."

Sammy is seven years old, the child of a Jewish mother and a black-militant father. He is normal in all respects, though he seems more popular with his friends than most children his age. Sammy's mother put him up for adoption when he was born. More than fifty foster families offered to take him in, and among them were Jews, Catholics, and Protestants. An agency finally placed Sammy in a Jewish home in Kew Gardens.

Myra is fifteen, the daughter of a well-to-do Jewish family in the Bronx. She is an attractive girl of higher than average intelligence who at the age of twelve began retreating into periods of complete silence. Two years ago she came to live at Pleasantville Cottage School, located in Westchester County some thirty miles outside New York City. Here she shares a cottage with twelve other girls, all of whom exhibited at one time or another some form of emotional disturbance or personality problem. At Pleasantville Myra receives psychiatric therapy and counseling. The doctor and caseworker are confident that she will eventually be able to return home permanently. On Friday nights all the cottages at Pleasantville have Sabbath candles burning.

Edward is nine years old. He is a retarded child, with evidence of damage to the central nervous system. For years his mother, who has two other children of normal intelligence, resisted the idea of giving Edward up to permanent medical care. But eventually it became obvious that the strain on the household might soon lead to his mother's nervous breakdown, and thus she sought assistance. He is enrolled at Edenwald, a Jewish school for retarded children housed on seventeen acres just outside the city.

What do these cases of children in trouble have in common?

They are representative of the cases that have been administered by the Jewish Child Care Association of New York, an agency which benefits thousands of Jewish families and Jewish children each year. At any given time, JCCA has in care between 1,400 and 1,500 children. The agency provides counseling, psychiatric diagnosis and therapy, vocational guidance, academic scholarships, remedial instruction, medical and dental care, and music, art, and dance lessons, among other services. It finds foster homes for children who need them and maintains treatment centers, such as Pleasantville Cottage School and Edenwald School. Each case that comes before the association is given individual attention, and all the facilities and services of the agency are put to use in order to secure the very best and most appropriate type of care for each child. JCCA's annual budget of more than $5 million is derived from an annual grant from the Federation of Jewish Philanthropies and is supplemented by city and state contributions. Private bequests are also used and some additional income is received through the Greater New York Fund. Even though the JCCA of New York works hand in hand with public welfare agencies and is itself no longer strictly sectarian, and even though there are many excellent and highly active Protestant and Catholic child-care agencies in New York, it has long been a tradition in the city that if you have to be a child in need, it is most advantageous, if it can possibly be arranged, to be Jewish.

Tammany Hall's beneficence augmented the power of its political leaders. The political functionary, working for the district leader, knew everyone who lived in his neighborhood and learned the domestic economy and social needs of each family. Of course, there were other help groups, the reformers and church people;

but they were perpetually stuck uptown; they were "there," the Tammany man was "here."

Often the Tammany man saved a family from disaster. The organization had a network of co-operating churches and Jewish organizations, and to these they referred people, according to the specific needs of each case. Usually they followed up to make sure the situation was corrected or at least improved. Families in need of coal, rent, food; boys in trouble with the cops; young men out of work; old men bedridden; and the troubled mother of the family—all could find assistance at the Tammany clubhouse.

The idea of the "settlement house" goes back to the problems engendered in London slums during the time of Queen Victoria. Intellectuals and reformers like John Ruskin, Matthew Arnold, and Arnold Toynbee urged university graduates to live among the urban poor and thereby elevate them. Before long, similar institutions were operating in the United States: Hull House in Chicago and the University Settlement, Henry Street Settlement, Greenwich House, Christodora House, and Madison House in New York. Supported in part by the city and partially staffed by non-Jewish volunteer workers, most of the financing for the New York houses was contributed by Jewish philanthropists—the Straus family, bankers James Speyer, Felix Warburg, Jacob Schiff, and others.

The Educational Alliance was the most famous of these. Its volunteer teachers included some of the city's most cultured Jews.

Out of the Alliance's classes came a long line of eminent citizens. David Sarnoff, radio and TV tycoon, learned English there, and so did his British counterpart, Sir Louis Stirling. Eddie Cantor's career began as an amateur entertainer at the Alliance's summer camp, and at the Alliance hall, Arthur Murray learned to dance. Morris Raphael Cohen tested his ideas as a youthful Alliance orator. It was during his membership at the Alliance that Sholom Aleichem wrote many of his works, lectured in the auditorium, and discussed literature and world Jewish themes with other members. Sir Jacob Epstein, Jo Davidson, Chaim Gross, William Auerbach-Levy, and Abraham Walkowitz paid three cents a lesson at the Alliance's art school. When Epstein was knighted, Walkowitz said to the sculptor's brother, "I see Jake is Sir Jake now." "Pfui," retorted the brother. "Jake was a knight

The Educational Alliance on the Lower East Side attracted all diverse elements of the area. An extremely tall, awkward adolescent named Arthur Murray Teichman learned to dance at the Alliance with such gratifying results that he made it his profession, a decision that eventually transformed him into Arthur Murray. Below, Arthur Murray and Hope Hampton.

at 102 Hester Street." Which is where Epstein had found his first models among pushcart peddlers.

The *Jewish Daily Forward* was *the* Yiddish-language newspaper of the Lower East Side. The *Forward*, one of five Yiddish-language papers, was founded in 1897, dedicated to helping the hundreds of thousands of Jewish immigrants, most of whom knew no English, to become familiar with their new country. It became soon

The press room of the *Jewish Daily Foreward* ("university of the immigrant for a penny").

enough not only the largest Yiddish-language paper in the United States, but for a long time the largest circulation newspaper in any foreign language as well. At the height of its popularity, the *Forward* had a circulation of almost 250,000 daily readers.

My father, who had brought us to America from Galicia in 1905, always said, "The *Jewish Daily Forward* is the university of the immigrant, a university which costs only a penny a day." My father, Reb Lebche, wrote the first sports story the *Forward* ever carried. It was probably the first sports story written in Yiddish in this country. He described the Jack Johnson-Jim Jeffries fight, explaining in the process not only what a heavyweight champion was, but how he delivered a one-two punch. My father assured the immigrants that boxing wasn't as savage as it appeared since a referee presided over the contestants who wore gloves.

The guiding spirit behind the *Forward* was Abraham Cahan, its editor for fifty years. He did more than run a university; he made the *Forward* the major weapon in the rise of the Jewish labor movement. An important segment of the American labor movement owes much, in some cases its very life, to the *Forward's* support of democratic and honest trade-unionism. It was Cahan and the *Forward* that mustered the brave vanguard of labor leaders who smashed the industrial jungle of the sweatshops. Today, the Workmen's Circle occupies a floor in the *Forward* building; this is an organization of some eight hundred chapters in the United States and Canada, with a membership of 75,000.

Cahan was a prolific writer in Yiddish and in English, and his novel, *The Rise of David Levinsky,* is the classic treatment of the Jewish immigrant's adjustment to American society, predating Mike Gold's *Jews Without Money* and by two full generations my own *Only in America.* Cahan envisioned the *Forward* as a mediator for immigrants, a mediator between Old World values and customs and New World values and customs. It was that vision which invested the *Forward* with its own unique values and traditions.

The *Forward* anticipated by fifty years the changes that would occur in American journalism. It was the first paper to introduce the magazine concept and the first to give extensive coverage to feature stories. It also offered its readers the first public available column of personal advice which its editors called the *Bintel Brief.* The *Bintel Brief* consisted of letters published for their general interest and help to the immigrant. The letters ran the gamut from the tragic to the comic:

"My little girl wants to pierce her ears for earrings. She says all the girls here have pierced ears, but my husband says no, that in America you do not pierce ears any more, but the girl is crying and tell my husband in the letter what is the best to do."

"My husband reads *The Forward*, but where does he read it? In the barbershop where he goes all the time with those other card players. Let him see this letter."

"Is it a sin to use face powder? Shouldn't a girl look beautiful? My father does not want me to use face powder. Is it a sin?"

Abraham Cahan emigrated to New York in 1882 where he remained until his death. In the early 1880s Cahan was greatly interested in organizing the immigrant Jewish workers using Yiddish as a medium for propaganda and helping to build Jewish labor unions "as the first step in getting these immigrants into the American labor movement." In 1902 he became editor of the *Jewish Daily Forward* which at that time had a circulation of 6,000. Under his guidance the paper reached its peak circulation of over 200,000. Cahan was the author of many works in English and in Yiddish. His novel in 1907, *The Rise of David Levinsky*, written in English, is generally considered an American classic. He also published many short stories. A pioneer in Yiddish journalism in America, Cahan has been a major factor in the Americanization of Jewish immigrants.

"My son is already twenty-six-years old and he doesn't want to get married. He says he is a Socialist and he is too busy. Socialism is Socialism, but getting married is important, too."

From the "Bintel Brief" to Dorothy Dix to "Dear Abby"—a history of American journalism in three "human-interest" installments.

The *Forward* is not privately owned. It is operated by a voluntary group of members, the Forward Association, membership in which is open to any trade unionist or follower of Democratic Socialism.

I remember another story my father contributed to the *Forward*, this one in the form of a lengthy letter: "The Yiddish press does not write enough material about America itself—the freedom of America. In Europe I was scared every time I met a Gentile on the street; and I went far out of my way to avoid passing a church. Here in America I pass a church, stop and examine the architecture and suddenly the priest comes out, and he smiles and says, 'Good morning,' to a bearded Jew. This is a development in the history of our people worth expanding into a whole series of articles. The priest smiles and says 'Good morning' because he's in America, too. It's America that made it better—not only better for me, a Jew, but also better for him, a priest."

As mentioned above, associated with the *Forward* was the Workmen's Circle, organized in 1892 to provide sick benefits and cemetery and funeral arrangements for Jewish factory workers. The organization is representative of the over-all labor-conscious sector in New York's Jewish life, and as such is part of the Jewish Labor Committee, which is the general aid agency of American Jewish trade-unionism.

The original Hebrew Trades Union, the *Jewish Daily Forward*, the Workmen's Circle, and the Jewish Labor Committee wielded important political influence in New York. These organizations, together with the International Ladies' Garment Workers, Amalgamated Clothing Workers, and Hat and Cap Makers, organized the political Liberal party in New York which now holds the balance of power in city elections. Often this vote provides the margin of a major party candidate's victory. It is interesting, for example, to note that the Republican (Protestant) Mayor John V. Lindsay won over Democrat (Jewish) Abraham Beame by the total vote of the Liberal party which had officially endorsed him.

Adolph Held, general manager of the *Jewish Daily Forward*.

When I was working on my biography of poet and Lincoln biographer Carl Sandburg, I came across a letter to Carl from fellow Socialist August Claessens. August was a Roman Catholic, but in his will requested that he be buried in the Workmen's Circle cemetery. Why? Because ". . . the last place the devil will look for a goy is in a Jewish cemetery."

Also buried in this cemetery are Abe Cahan, Sholom Aleichem, and the 145 boys and girls who died in the Triangle Shirtwaist Factory fire.

The first organized Jewish philanthropic organization in America was established in 1822 by leaders of Shearith Israel. German Jews organized a Hebrew Benevolent Society, which by the early 1850s was helping two hundred people a year.

The first appeal to all Jews to contribute to a fund for needy immigrants came as early as 1837 when there was a door to door soliciation for food, clothing, fuel, and cash.

In 1839 the New York Hebrew Assistance Society was created to aid immigrants. Old-line Jews sponsored a benefit concert of Italian opera in a Christian church in 1849 to raise funds for the relief of newly arriving German Jews. Organization of the Bachelors Hebrew Benevolent Loan Society, the Young Men's Hebrew Benevolent Fuel Association, and a host of other mutual aid societies between 1830 and 1855 demonstrated that the principle and

The headquarters of Brith Abraham on Seventh Street on the Lower East Side of New York.

practice of Jewish-Americans caring for their own had become the bedrock on which Jewish communal life was being built.

Out of the mutual aid societies grew the first fraternal orders and cultural groups. B'nai B'rith, the oldest national Jewish membership organization, was founded in New York in 1843, mostly by German Jews, who also established the Free Sons of Israel in 1849 and the United Order of True Sisters, the first women's organization independent of the synagogue, in 1852. These fraternal societies were important instruments for Americanizing the immigrants and for giving them social, economic and cultural opportunities.

In 1874 the United Hebrew Charities was founded through an amalgamation of the old Hebrew Benevolent Society and four smaller groups. The new organization created the Hebrew Sheltering Guardian Society in 1879 to care for needy children and a year later established the Hebrew Technical School for Girls. Through subsequent mergers, the United Hebrew Charities emerged in 1917 as the Federation of Jewish Philanthropies, a huge philanthropic and social welfare complex, which, in the 1960s alone, has poured $150 million into the maintenance of some 116 institutions and has spent tens of millions more on new facilities.

The Home for Aged and Infirm Hebrews, the first of its kind, opened in 1870. Four years later the native-born and German-

The Hebrew Free
Loan Society.

Jewish leadership founded the Ninety-second Street YM-YWHA,
now the country's oldest existing Jewish community center, to
provide cultural and recreational activities for young people.
Montefiore Hospital was established in 1884 as an outgrowth of
a home for chronic invalids established by Mount Sinai and the
United Hebrew Charities to cope with the growing number of
chronically ill who refused to go to city institutions.

Because of deep-seated religious differences, immense social
and cultural cleavages, and wide economic disparities between
the older community and the masses of Eastern Europeans who
arrived after 1880, there grew up two separate if parallel Jewish
communities. Many uptowners were contemptuous of and sometimes hostile to the zealous efforts of their Yiddish-speaking
downtown coreligionists to recreate Old World institutions, to
maintain the minutiae of Orthodoxy, and to cling to their own
folkways. The Eastern Europeans equated the Reform synagogues
and even modernized Orthodox congregations with churches and
regarded the Americanized Jew as a thinly disguised Christian
missionary. In turn, many of the German Jews denigrated the
newcomers as "uncouth strangers" who threatened the status of
the older community by giving impetus to the rising anti-alien
sentiment.

It was not until the Hitler era that all such differences were finally washed away. Each group realized that to the surrounding Christian society, a Jew is a Jew; the non-Jewish community does not give religious tests, nor does it distinguish between a Jew whose ancestors had fought with General Washington in 1776 and a Jew who arrived from Czechoslovakia yesterday. A united Jewish community was still a necessity.

The social-action and charitable organizations maintain individual directorships and methods; but today, Jews of New York and of America are more or less united in all philanthropic, social-action, and defense activities. And except for a mere handful, they are united in their deep concern for the safety and success of Israel.

Since 1949 the New York Association for New Americans, an agency of the United Jewish Appeal, has helped more than 130,000 refugees from Europe and the Arab countries—this at a cost of more than one million dollars. The association finds jobs for the newcomers and provides training, education, and intensive English language study for all those who need such assistance. A workshop for the aged and handicapped is a part of the agency's operations. Settlement aid, which is offered to all arriving families, consists of many services including medical and dental care, clothing, school placement, and a business and loan program.

A special youth services program, emphasizing language study, financial help, and social interaction, has helped nine hundred

The Hebrew Actors Union, founded by Boris Thomashefsky, the great Yiddish actor. The Union was a forerunner of Actors' Equity.

185

young newcomers in the past five years. This program also supplies college scholarships and directs young people to temporary or part-time employment.

Many of these immigrants, who have had harsh experiences in Arab countries or in Europe during the last several years, express dramatic reactions to the association's aid programs. "For the first time in my life, somebody helped me because I was a Jew" was a response representative of the feelings of many of these newcomers. Another striking feature of the new life these people have adopted is the opportunity in New York City for living freely, openly, and even proudly as Jews. "People in this city get a holiday on Passover and talk about it as though it were the most natural thing in the world."

Dore Schary, motion picture producer and playwright. Schary won the Antoinette Perry award for his play *Sunrise at Campobello*. He was national chairman of the Anti-Defamation League of the B'nai B'rith, 1963–69, and was also involved in the Citizens Crusade Against Poverty.

Among the motion pictures he wrote or produced were *Boys Town* (Academy award), *Edison the Man, Joe Smith, American, Journey for Margaret, I'll Be Seeing You, The Farmer's Daughter, The Bachelor and the Bobby-Soxer, Till the End of Time, Bad Day at Black Rock, The Last Hunt,* and *Designing Woman*.

Billy Rose and his wife Joyce Matthews. Billy Rose was a shorthand champion and in 1918 was Bernard M. Baruch's stenographer at the War Industries Board in Washington. His great success came as a theatrical producer, and in 1937 he directed the Aquacades at the Great Lakes Exposition in Cleveland and two years later at the New York World's Fair.

He later operated Billy Rose's Diamond Horseshoe, a cabaret in New York City and was the president of several theatrical corporations.

David Belasco, producer, actor, and playwright, whose life is the story of the American stage. Considered without equal in his day as a creator of new talent and of revolutionary stage effects, he made famous such stars as Mrs. Leslie Carter, Frances Starr, David Warfield, and Lenore Ulric. Mary Pickford graduated from the Belasco school to become "America's sweetheart." Belasco produced 400 plays, the works of some 125 authors including 150 dramas of his own. His stage production of *Madame Butterfly* inspired Puccini to compose his great opera. Puccini also made into an opera *The Girl of the Golden West,* Belasco's own work, and in 1910 the world premiere was held at the Metropolitan Opera House with Toscanini conducting and Enrico Caruso, Pasquale Amato, and Emmy Destinn in the chief roles.

Paul Muni. One evening while Muni was playing on the Yiddish stage, the great Broadway actor John Barrymore came down to see this new phenomenon. Muni was playing the part of an old rabbi, and Barrymore went backstage and said he would like to see the old gent. Suddenly Paul Muni took off his beard, put on his skates, and skated out of the room; he was seventeen years old at the time. He brought to life such famous men as Louis Pasteur and Emile Zola in motion pictures and played Clarence Darrow in *Inherit the Wind*.

Eddie Cantor was educated in the New York public schools and at eighteen
made his debut on amateur night at Miner's Bowery Theater. He
subsequently joined a burlesque show, worked as a singing waiter at
Coney Island and in 1916 first appeared in a musical comedy on the Pacific
Coast where he was noticed by Florenz Ziegfeld and was brought to New
York to appear in *The Midnight Frolics.* He became a featured player
in the *Ziegfeld Follies*, appeared in *Broadway Brevities* (1920), and
*Make It Snappy* (1922); he starred in *Kid Boots* from 1923 to 1926. In
1926 he made his first appearance in motion pictures in *Kid Boots,* starring
later in *Special Delivery, Whoopee, Palmy Days, Kid from Spain, Roman
Scandals, Kid Millions, Strike Me Pink,* and many others.

# CHAPTER 10

# "A Charge in the Coming Winter"

AMERICA HAS BEEN GOOD to the Jews, although anti-Semitism has happened here, too.

One of the original twenty-three Jewish settlers in the city was Asser Levy, the first Jewish champion of civil rights. A year after his arrival, Levy (whose entire name was Asser Levy van Swellem, indicating a residence in Schwelm, Westphalia) sent a petition to city officials asking for the right to stand guard like all the other non-Jewish citizens and thus be relieved, if he so chose, of the heavy taxes imposed upon Jews to support the sentries. The Dutch authorities denied Levy's petition and told him, in effect, that if he didn't like it here, he could go back where he came from.

But Levy persisted in his arguments. He appealed his case to the mother country, Holland, and he won. His perseverance finally admitted the Jewish settlers as first-class citizens of the growing city.

In 1907 Henry James, the Anglo-American novelist, remarked that he was shocked at "the Hebrew conquest of New York," which he feared would transform the city into "a new Jerusalem." A year later Police Commissioner Theodore A. Bingham charged that New York's one million Jews, representing a fourth of the total city population, accounted for half the city's crime. Confronted with the statistics which disproved his thesis, Bingham retracted, apologized, and resigned.

These are indicative of the minor disturbances on the surface of Jewish-American life. More interesting and more significant have been the measures taken by the Anglo-Saxon majority to safeguard their position and their illusions. Let us look into the background of these manifestations.

In significant ways the Jews and America were made for each other. No other nation values individual effort so highly as the United States. The virtue of hard work, plus inventiveness and intelligence (long considered Jewish specialties), as the means to happiness and success is nowhere so exalted as in this country; it is, or was until recently, every American boy's dream to rise socially and economically on the basis of his own merit and initiative, with nothing extraneous to bar his progress. In America this ethic of success through individual effort, with its inevitable emphasis upon success in business, enjoyed for years the status of a religion. Americans guard this freedom of opportunity more zealously than the priests of antiquity guarded the chastity of their vestal virgins. To this day many of our state governors run for office on the grounds that they will run the state on sound business principles; many of our Presidents have won elections on the same grounds; and the national government as a whole is often judged in terms of corporate standards. One of the most successful best-sellers in the history of American publishing was Bruce Barton's *The Man Nobody Knows,* which in the 1920s portrayed Jesus Christ as the founder of modern business. About the same time the Metropolitan Casualty Insurance Company issued a pamphlet which claimed that Moses was one of the greatest salesmen and real estate promoters who ever lived.

Theoretically, the Jews, who have always been noted for their ambition and know-how in financial affairs, would seem to be ideal citizens of the American republic. No doubt many European Jews responded enthusiastically and energetically to the American doctrine of success, and indeed it was this that brought them to America in the first place to try their own luck. For a time, all went well. The Jews seemed to be adept practitioners of one of the basic American values; and as such they commanded admiration, according to a logic that the circumstances forced upon even those most resistant to accepting it. In 1913 a large circulation magazine, *McClure's,* carried a series about Abraham Cahan with the title "That Wonderful Machine, the Jewish Brain." In the series, the editors predicted that someday the Semitic influence would dominate America, so compatible was the coming-together of natural (Jewish) human aptitude on the one hand, and national goals and ideals on the other.

Then a reaction against the Jews set in, partly sparked by the widespread labor strikes that followed World War I, strikes which many observers believed were inspired by radical Jewish immigrants on New York's Lower East Side. During this same period America suffered a rash of bombings and bomb scares, which politicians were prompt to associate with foreigners, immigrants, and radical agitators. The super-patriots and "pure American" groups rose up as if in answer to these troubles. Jews, Negroes, and Catholics were lumped together as undesirables. President Coolidge composed an article for another large-circulation magazine on the dangers of race-pollution in America, and Henry Ford began printing his virulent anti-Semitic pamphlets in Dearborn. Many Jews, along with other aliens of all descriptions, were deported; stricter immigration laws were passed, with drastically reduced quotas allowed from Eastern and Southern Europe.

Meanwhile, even the less hysterical elements in the American Establishment were also reacting against minority groups. The Big Business elite was frightened, not so much by the Jews' radical activities as by their prospects for achievement in Big Business. There was also the new notion of the "business communion." In practice, it meant that a corporation chose to employ only those people who came from the same backgrounds and shared perhaps the same prejudices as management. This sort of polite exclusion implied nothing against the Jews as Jews; they simply did not fit in the Big Business Establishment. Burton Hendrick's book *The Jews in America*, popular during the 1920s and influential thereafter, argued the thesis that the Jews and Big Business were basically incompatible. Chester Bernard's pseudo-scientific study *The Functions of the Executive* made the same point and a long-lasting impression, discussing the importance of "communion" among business colleagues.

One result of this attitude was to limit by law the immigration of European Jews to America and to exclude American Jews from social life and Big Business, both of which the Protestant elite dominated. This ban, in truth, was never 100 per cent effective nor was it permanent. Legislation passed in 1965 has liberalized the immigration quotas, and the technological advances and the phenomenal industrial growth of the past twenty years have demanded the acceptance of qualified Jews, as well as members of other minority groups, into key positions.

But for a major portion of the twentieth century, Jews lived within a quota system, with only so many admitted to college, only so many to medical school, only so many advanced in the postal service, only so many licensed to sell insurance. The system was perhaps unconsciously copied from the quota system enacted by the United States Government to control foreign immigration.

Congress passed the first restrictive immigration law in 1917, authorizing the Department of Labor to deport aliens implicated in radicalism no matter how long they had lived in the United States before the supposed crime. In deportation, the nativist, the American xenophobe, held the ultimate weapon against the foreign-born dissenter. Thousands of immigrants were arrested on the street, detained without a hearing, and returned to the country of their birth, leaving behind forever wives, children, and small histories.

The father of restrictive immigration was Albert Johnson, a newspaperman from the state of Washington whose twenty-year career in Congress from 1912 to 1932 was devoted to closing the gates. In 1919 he proposed a bill which would limit immigration from European countries to 5 per cent of the number of foreign-born of each nationality present in the United States at the time of the census in 1910. Woodrow Wilson vetoed the bill, but the urge for restrictive immigration was too strong.

In collaboration with Senator David A. Reed, Johnson produced another, more stringent bill which limited immigration to *2 per cent* of the nationalities present in the United States at *the time of the census of 1890*. The bill aimed at controlling racial qualities. The bulk of Americans in 1890 were from northern Europe. The bill penalized Italians, Slavs, Jews, and Greeks. It allowed a total immigration of 270,000, dividing the admission of these immigrants under a quota assigned to each country. Thus, 60,000 Englishmen could emigrate—and 308 Greeks.

The immigration quotas which were passed by the Congress after World War I had grievous implications for the Jews of Europe during the years of the Nazi holocaust. The quota system meant that the United States could offer sanctuary to only 168,000 Jews fleeing Adolf Hitler. W. H. Auden sang a dirge set to the blues rhythms which described the tragic plight of these people left to face their oppressors:

Went to a committee; they offered me a chair;
Asked me politely to return next year;
But where shall we go today, my dear, but where shall we go today?

Came to a public meeting; the speaker got up and said:
"If we let them in, they will steal our daily bread";
He was talking of you and me, my dear, he was talking of you and me.

Thought I heard the thunder rumbling in the sky;
It was Hitler over Europe, saying: "They must die";
We were in his mind, my dear, we were in his mind.

Saw a poodle in a jacket fastened with a pin,
Saw a door opened and a cat let in:
But they weren't German Jews, my dear, but they weren't German Jews. . . .

Walked through a wood, saw the birds in the trees;
They had no politicians and sang at their ease:
They weren't the human race, my dear, they weren't the human race.

Dreamed I saw a building with a thousand floors,
A thousand windows and a thousand doors;
Not one of them was ours, my dear, not one of them was ours.

Stood on a great plain in the falling snow;
Ten thousand soldiers marched to and fro:
Looking for you and me, my dear, looking for you and me.


But I must not leave the reader with the impression that I believe the anti-Semitism of the 1930s was all-pervasive. Under Franklin D. Roosevelt, this nation underwent a vast change, a change which transformed America. Before Roosevelt's administrations, the United States was largely composed of a small-town-based electorate which aspired to little more than individual success in business and social acceptance at the local country club. But with the population drift toward the cities, the nation gradually became predominantly composed of urban voters who represented an ethnic mixture oriented towards collective and political goals—for the simple reason that success, power, and acceptance had been denied to them on an individual level.

Was this, to use the popular and possibly the ultimately important criterion, good for the Jews or bad for the Jews? Historians tell us that during the period 1900–30 the major drama enacted on the stage of the American continent was this population drift towards the cities, and that this drift consisted largely of immigrants from Europe and Negroes and poor whites from rural America. This influx merged into what the social scientists call the Urban Frontier, and F.D.R. was its new hero. What it meant is really difficult to grasp, even today. But Catholics, Jews, Negroes, and other minority groups felt that they had been given a new lease on life, that the old familiar phrases from the Pledge of Allegiance, the Declaration of Independence, and the U. S. Constitution acquired a new and revitalized meaning. Under Roosevelt, these minority groups felt encouraged to participate as never before in American politics and society. F.D.R. appointed Italians, Irish, Catholics, Jews, and Negroes to governmental positions of importance.

Although discrimination against the Jews continued throughout the Great Depression, by the end of the thirties, studies showed that the Jews had achieved a high level of education and prosperity in America. Ironically, they were closest statistically to the occupational achievements of the Episcopalians and Presbyterians—whom Jews thought had kept them out of the really lucrative professions.

The nation was split over Roosevelt as his tenure in office continued, as today it is split over our foreign policy. The American rich began to hate F.D.R. He was associated in the minds of conservatives with unpopular ethnic groups, and partly for this reason and partly because his economic reforms penalized the plutocracy, F.D.R. became a symbol of democracy run mad.

In 1947 *The Amboy Dukes*, Irving Shulman's classic story of Brooklyn's Jewish street gangs, revealed its ethnic dimension honestly in its use of the family names of its gang members. It was a moving account of brutal life on the streets of Brownsville, based primarily on Shulman's own observations and partially on a true incident involving the death of a Brooklyn school teacher at the hands of two students. Some of the city's influential Jewish

Barbra Streisand, recording artist and star of Broadway and Hollywood.

leaders were upset about the "image" of Jewish boys projected in Shulman's novel, and when the Avon paperback edition was released in 1949 the result of this anxiety was evident in the polyglot ethnic names inserted by Shulman in place of the original Jewish patronymics; and several sections of the book that had given a particularly Jewish identification to the characters or incidents were deleted. Shulman says that he acceded to the request for these changes from the reprint publisher because at the time he was a struggling young writer with an interest in getting as much exposure as possible. For the Bantam edition of the 1960s, however, Shulman was no longer a boy, and he insisted that the ethnic slant be restored and that the story be allowed to stand or fall within its original context.

A tip of my yarmulkah to Irving Shulman. I am reminded of the Jewish businessmen who advised me not to reopen the Leo Frank case in my book *A Little Girl Is Dead*—out of fear that old grievances might be reactivated, old wounds reopened. To them I said, as I say to Shulman's censors, *fear is no answer to the anti-Semites.*

One of the most interesting conclusions on the subject of anti-Semitism in America comes from a recent study financed by the Anti-Defamation League (ADL) and conducted by the University of California. The study showed that the Christian religion played a major role, and continues to play a major role, in the development of anti-Semitism. Church-going Protestants and Catholics were asked to respond to such statements as "The Jews can never

Irving M. Engel in 1955 brought the great American Jewish Committee into the civil rights movement on behalf of the Negroes.

be forgiven for what they did to Jesus until they accept Him as the True Saviour" and "The reason the Jews have so much trouble is because God is punishing them for rejecting Jesus," etc. The questionnaire was circulated in the San Francisco Bay area. Although many of the answers revealed a high proportion of "disagree" replies, it is clear that a substantial number of the people questioned believe such pronouncements to be true. And such religious beliefs lead to secular anti Semitism—various deeds, actions, comments, and so forth, directed against Jews every day in our predominantly *non*-religiously oriented society.

Related studies have shown that the more education an individual has, the less he tends to be anti-Semitic, and that the better Christians get to know Jews, the more friendly they are toward them. Contact with Jews is an important factor in reducing anti-Jewish prejudice. In the area of politics, discrimination appears to be lessening. Whereas in 1945 approximately one fourth of the people questioned in a survey said that they would vote for a candidate because he was openly anti-Semitic, in the 1960s only 5 per cent stated that they would do so. At the same time, the proportion of the population that expresses an indifferent reaction to anti-Semitism remains about the same, and it is a considerable proportion.

Anti-Semitism has shown a few new wrinkles in recent years, chief among which is of course the emergence of black-extremist anti-Jewish sentiment. The Black Panthers claim a racial identification with the Arabs and undying hostility to Israel and all Zionists everywhere. The Puerto Ricans of New York join in this absurdity (as if the Arabs were other than Semites). One unforeseen consequence of all the virulent talk among these groups is the embarrassment of whites on the liberal left, particularly in California and New York; they must either disavow their affiliation with the underprivileged blacks, pretend ignorance of black anti-Semitism, or join in the chorus which blames the Jews for America's exploitation of the Negro, and Israel for the abuse of the Arabs and Jordan. Unfortunately a large number of good men on the left have chosen the last alternative.

During the past forty years or so New York City has witnessed several epidemics of the anti-Semitic virus. In the late 1930s and early 1940s the German-American Bund promoted the beating of Jewish kids on New York's sidewalks; and in a nine-week period from December 1959 to February 1960, the city suffered from the effects of the swastika-painting outbreak, which had hit West Germany at the same time and left its mark on many other American cities as well. Along with the swastikas painted on synagogues and shop fronts were anti-Jewish slogans, threatening phone calls, obscene letters, broken windows, and other malice and vandalism. The entire wave of incidents was triggered by the appearance of a swastika on the wall of the synagogue in Cologne, Germany. In the United States the despoilers (more than 160 were apprehended) for the most part turned out to be adolescent boys—80 per cent were in the age group nine to eighteen. Many of these kids were not fully aware of the meaning of what they were doing—they had seen the swastikas pictured on TV, and the painting seemed an exciting and at the same time a rebellious action. But investigations also revealed a fairly high proportion of neo-Nazi organization members among the guilty; their groups had leaders and by-laws, souvenirs of Hitler's Germany, flags, firearms, helmets, boots. . . .

The most recent eruption of anti-Semitism in New York City occurred during the teachers' strike of 1968 and 1969. Here the basic problem was the question of who should administer and teach the school children of the black sections of the city—black teachers or white? A majority of New York's white teachers and school administrators are Jewish, many of them having devoted long years of hard work to the system, which promotes individual workers on a merit-seniority basis.

Now the blacks wanted self-rule in their own districts; and instead of attacking ills in the system or singling out certain teachers and administrators as incompetent or unsympathetic or unsuited to their positions, they launched a campaign against the Jews, claiming that the Jewish educational establishment was poisoning the minds of black children. Abusive comments against Jews were broadcast over New York radio stations and anti-Semitic leaflets were distributed at rallies and demonstrations. Threatening letters, anonymous phone calls, exhortations to the black community to boycott or disrupt Jewish business establishments—all these symptoms of the anti-Semitic virus contributed to the pollution of New York's already polluted atmosphere. Worse, there was evidence that young blacks were being taught to hate the Jews by hardened, older, professional hate-mongers. Jewish organizations and agencies meantime accused the city administration of favoritism toward the blacks, while the blacks accused the city administration of favoritism toward the Jews.

What anti-Semitism has done in this instance is to obscure what is a crucial and fundamental issue, one which only men of good will can resolve. The blacks and Puerto Ricans are right: their children will learn immeasurably more and become good citizens more quickly if they have pride in their origin, which black and Puerto Rican teachers can more easily inspire in them. It is, however, cruel to banish from a profession and from a classroom Jewish men and women who have conscientiously served for many years. My sympathy goes to the men who must decide upon this resolution. I do not think the epithets "nigger" and "kike" help expand this dialogue reasonably.

The oppressed seeking relief lash out against the weakest link in the white power structure; that link is often the Jews. In the early sit-ins in the South, the Negro's first point of attack for integration was the Jewish department store or the Jewish-run restaurant, even when it happened that these businesses were the smallest establishments on Main Street.

The labor unions have also made use of this strategy. In Gas-

Rabbi Arthur J. Lelyveld, the president of the American Jewish Congress, wages unceasing efforts in the areas of law and social action.

tonia, North Carolina, which has over one hundred cotton mills, the only unionized plants are those owned by Jews. The Jewish millowner is no more amenable to unionism than the Christian, but he is more vulnerable.

The Jewish Defense League was founded in 1968 by an Orthodox rabbi, Meir Kahane, who at the time wrote a column for the Brooklyn *Jewish Press*. It is obviously a militant and violence-prone organization—the Jews' answer to the Black Panthers. Yet its charter members insist that it is also based on high idealism. Although the JDL's primary function is action to combat anti-Semitism, which members believe means answering physical attacks in kind, JDL leaders are motivated as well by the so-called Revisionist Zionist movement and also by a crusading zeal to free Russian Jews from Soviet anti-Semitism.

Critics of the movement, and there are many in Jewish agencies, point out that the JDL's fear of anti-Semitism in the United States is exaggerated and paranoid. There have also been occasions, these same critics observe, when the JDL appeared on the scene ready to do battle when no battle was intended by presumed anti-Jewish groups.

In reply, members of the JDL gesture with some pride toward the good work they have accomplished and continue to accomplish in safeguarding their neighborhoods. For many months, elderly Jews in the so-called frontier neighborhoods were molested on their way to shop or synagogue, and the militant youths of the JDL came to their assistance by providing an armed escort in these high-crime areas of the city. Today the movement claims a national membership of several thousand with chapters in a dozen or more cities of the East and on many college campuses. Proud, somewhat nervous, anti-Establishment, and impatient with slower moving, legalistic and verbalistic liberal organizations, the JDL attracts many young people who might otherwise join some of the more familiar radical political groups which have become a force in contemporary American life. The rallying cry of the JDL, in reference to the Nazi atrocities against Jews, is "Never again!"

The Jewish Defense League's 1970–71 activities drew comment in fifty Jewish newspapers, each of which denounced JDL tactics as disgraceful and a cause for concern.

The group was castigated for diverting attention from legiti-

mate grievances of the Jews in the Soviet Union by creating un-
due sympathy for harassed Soviet citizens here, for jeopardizing
the status of the Soviet Mission to the United Nations, and for
threatening Soviet-American relations.

The Anti-Defamation League said: "We look with growing
consternation upon the anarchistic barbarism of JDL tactics. The
Jewish Defense League is a self-appointed group of vigilantes
whose help the Jewish community does not need or want."

In summation, let me say that anti-Semitism in America has
two forms, one social, one religious. The social form of anti-
Semitism depends upon exclusivity—barring Jews from membership in certain institutions, from living in certain neighborhoods,
and from attending certain schools.

There have been hotels which advertised "restricted clientele,"
meaning Jews were not allowed to register. The Catskill Mountains in New York, known as a famous Jewish summer resort area,
became what it is because half a century ago some rich Jews
were not permitted to register at existing hotels there. They
banded together and built their own hotels.

There are city clubs in many American towns to this day whose
members simply refuse to admit a Jew. The city club or the downtown club is where businessmen entertain their clients and their
customers. This may at first seem more an inconvenience for a
Jew than a deprivation. But many national firms realize they cannot appoint a Jew as their regional representative because discrimination will exclude him from certain community affairs and
a lot of business is transacted through the community.

The infamous "gentleman's agreement" is a tacit understanding
among the residents of a neighborhood that no one will rent or
sell a home to a Jew. There are still realtors who boast to prospective home buyers, "Our town is a Jew-free town."

Although Albert Lasker, who transformed the advertising industry was a Jew, for many years agencies simply refused to hire
a Jew in any capacity. Jews began to succeed in advertising when
they founded their own agencies and lured Jewish clients to
them.

None of these practices ever had sanction in law. All of them
today are expressly against the law.

Religious anti-Semitism centers on the charge that the Jews
killed Christ. The charge is inaccurate. The Romans executed

Christ by crucifixion. Still the charge persists. There's little the Jews can do about it. Even if they wanted to, they could not accept the collective guilt for an event which happened nearly two thousand years ago.

From this charge, needless and absurd though it is, grow many others. Gentiles have charged the Jews with ritual murder, with having all the money, with Communism, with sticking together, with pushing in the subway. The truth is that if you level one charge a man cannot rebut, you can level millions.

# CHAPTER 11

# Bagels and Halos

THE GERMAN-JEWISH POET Heinrich Heine is commemorated in a small park on the Grand Concourse in the Bronx by a monument originally intended for his native Düsseldorf. Düsseldorf refused the monument partly for political and partly for anti-Semitic reasons. Other German cities also refused the memorial. Finally a group of German-Americans, Gentiles as well as Jews, raised the money to pay for and transport the statue to New York for its unveiling in 1899. Today a synagogue stands at one end of the park, while a Catholic school occupies space at the other end. In between, the legendary Lorelei entwine themselves around Heine's graven image in a timeless gesture celebrating the triumph of humane appreciation over prejudice.

In New York the Loyal League of Yiddish Sons of Erin marches each year in the St. Patrick's Day parade.

A market in Spanish Harlem displays the sign SE HABLA YIDDISH.

The First Israel Bank and Trust Company of New York has a convenient Christmas Club plan for its depositors.

Pablo Casals, who is ninety-six years old and descended from Catholic parents, tells the orchestras he conducts to "play Jewish." When questioned once about his meaning, Casals replied: "My own life has been so enriched by tender associations with Jewish fellow artists and friends. What people on earth have contributed more to human culture than the Jewish people? They have so much heart—yes, and head too! So when I am conducting and tell the orchestra to 'play Jewish,' they know what I mean."

No book about the Jews of the modern world would be complete without some reference to Pope John XXIII, who is remembered by all the world for his humanity and compassion. Under the provisions of Vatican Council II, which Pope John directed, the Catholic Church took historic steps toward correcting certain wrongs to the Jews both stated and implied in Church doctrine, as well as speaking out for greater understanding and tolerance among members of all Christian sects. The articles of the Vatican II speak of "the spiritual bond linking the people of the New Covenant with Abraham's stock" and elsewhere emphasize the common fatherhood of both Christians and Jews. When a group of Jewish spokesmen called upon Pope John in the early 1960s he greeted them with the words, "I am Joseph your brother." John's attitudes created an interfaith spirit of good will that prevails to this day; in fact, because of his influence, there are doings afoot in New York's five boroughs that constitute a veritable revolution in Catholic-Jewish relations.

The bulk of this activity focuses on education in Catholic parochial schools; but it also includes interfaith dialogues, addresses, publications, and seminars conducted on the university level at both Catholic and Jewish institutions. Whereas a decade ago interfaith meetings consisted largely of tea-socials or banquets with carefully prepared menus, today Catholic, Jewish, and some Protestant clergymen are participating in activities designed to increase understanding and influence attitudes by means of basic and highly practical procedures. Bishops, rabbis, monsignors, priests, ministers, seminary students, scholars, and other laymen are forming councils, commissions, and study programs which will bring people of the major faiths together as never before. Guidelines in this direction have been established for American bishops, and a Catholic-Jewish Relations Committee has been set up in New York for the purpose of implementing a number of specific projects, which include Catholic seminars on Judaism.

Perhaps the most important and far-reaching interfaith activity has been the preparation of a series of pamphlets, books, and filmstrips produced jointly by the Catholic Archdiocese of New York and the Anti-Defamation League of B'nai B'rith. Study after study

has shown that prejudice is to a large extent (though not ex-
clusively) a product of ignorance, legend, unsubstantiated belief, misunderstanding, fear, and a general lack of knowledge. In order to provide the sort of knowledge that might reduce prejudice, the Catholic Archdiocese and the ADL are sending out information about Jews in America, in literature, and in world history, including for example specimens of writing that emerged from the Nazi holocaust and stereotypes of the Jew in English drama and fiction. This is no halfhearted effort, but a full-fledged campaign. In 1968 New York's 7,900 Catholic parochial school teachers viewed a series of closed-circuit television programs on Judaism and the Jews, with the idea that these faculty would pass on their increased understanding to their classes. The potential impact of this program is enormous. New York's archdiocesan schools alone have an enrollment exceeding 372,000; and the series has been made available for distribution to all other Catholic school systems throughout the nation.

All over the New York area, in the five boroughs, in Westchester County, in Rockville Center, Jamaica, and elsewhere, interfaith groups consisting of Jews and Catholics, and not excluding certain Protestant sects, are setting up and maintaining dialogues, colloquiums, seminars, dinners, discussion groups, "think-ins," and "happenings" for the purpose of increasing harmony and understanding among the faiths, and for planning projects for social action as well. Bagels and halos are coming together and interlocking, with benefits for all men and women who wish to make real the basic concepts of American democracy and at the same time to work together on some of the overwhelming problems of our time.


Five thousand black Jews live in New York City, most of whom trace their ancestry back to the West Indies and ultimately to Africa. In the sixteenth century Jews fleeing persecution in Portugal and Spain, as Marranos, left their native countries and came to the West Indies. Black servants working in the homes of these Jewish exiles sometimes adopted the Jewish religion. Living for the most part in Harlem, the East Bronx, Williamsburg, and Bedford-Stuyvesant, they constitute the membership of New York's black synagogues.

Generally uneasy about the Black Jew designation, these New Yorkers talk instead about belonging to the Sephardic tradition

—originating in Spain, Portugal, Tunis, and Morocco. Says one young Sephardic, who is married to a white girl from Israel, "I don't have to consider myself colored just because others do. I am a Jew, and color has nothing to do with that. I am a Jew of Hispanic ancestry."

Rabbi Wentworth Matthew, leader of Harlem's Commandment-Keeper's Congregation and generally acknowledged as the first black rabbi in the city, describes his followers as Ethiopian Hebrews, linked in some way to the Falashas of Ethiopia—black Jews who once ruled their own territory within that kingdom and who professed literal adherence to the Old Testament.

The black Jews of New York are predominantly Orthodox in practice, and many of them keep kosher kitchens. On the Sabbath they travel only to go to and from prayer at the temple, to use the phone, or to cook. The males are circumcised. "Orthodoxy," says Rabbi Matthew, "is the one concept that remains uniform and does not differ in practice from congregation to congregation." Matthew is seventy-six and a native of Lagos, Nigeria. He says his congregation accepts a child as Jewish so long as one parent is Jewish. "The white Jews are more restrictive," he says. "The mother has to be Jewish for the child to be considered a Jew."

According to the American Jewish Committee, their program *Hatzaad horishon*, the first step toward communication between black and white Jews, serves the needs of black Jews as Jews rather than as blacks. But "We are not seeking intermarriage with white Jews, nor are we eager to lose our identity among the whites," says Rabbi Matthew. One of the rabbi's students, Mrs. Esther Bibbins, adds, "We are proud to be both black and Jewish." Recently, Hatzaad was given a grant of ten thousand dollars by the Federation of Jewish Philanthropies to further the work of encouraging black Jews to use the health, welfare, and educational facilities of New York's over-all Jewish community.

Not all Jewish organizations have been willing to recognize the black group. The National Board of Rabbis has no black members. Fifteen years ago Matthew applied for membership on the board, but his application was rejected. "He didn't have the credentials," explains Rabbi Harold Gordon, executive vice president of the board. This means Matthew was not ordained by a recognized rabbinical school or by a recognized rabbi.

The black Jews of New York seem to relate without friction to Gentile blacks. "If my friends invite me to their home," says one black Jewish lady, "and it happens to be Friday night, I just tell them I can't make it, and they change the invitation to another night."

How did these New Yorkers, with children in public schools, react to the recent teachers' strike? Generally, the opinion of the black Jews is that the black Ocean Hill-Brownsville governing board is right. "They are Jewish teachers teaching black kids," they say. "It is unfortunate that the teachers happen to be Jewish."

Rose Pastor Stokes, labor agitator, writer, artist, Socialist, pioneer, and unflinching fighter in every phase of the struggle for human progress.

Born in Poland, she helped her mother sew bows on ladies' slippers in the ghetto of East London. A few years later the family came to the United States and settled in Cleveland where, at the age of eleven, she entered a cigar factory, becoming the breadwinner for the family, educating herself while working. At the age of twenty she began to contribute a weekly column to the *Jewish Daily News* in New York City and while covering an assignment for the paper she met Graham Phelps Stokes, of the famous American family and a millionaire, whom she married. She worked for many years for Margaret Sanger in the birth control movement and she was the outstanding leader in the hotel and restaurant strike of 1912. Later she was a leading figure in the ladies shirtwaist makers strike. An active member of the Socialist party for years, she was active in the League for Industrial Democracy, lecturing throughout the United States. She was a prolific writer and her outstanding poem, *Patterson,* is a labor classic. She also translated Morris Rosenfeld's songs of labor from Yiddish.

In 1929, during a demonstration in New York City protesting the oppression of the people of Haiti, she was struck with a club by a policeman. The bruise developed complications of which she died four years later.

Lionel Trilling, professor of English at Columbia University and an eminent American critic.

Norman Podhoretz . . . from Cambridge to *Commentary*.

Mr. and Mrs. Oscar S. Straus. Oscar S. Straus, jurist, diplomat, merchant, and philanthropist. United States ambassador to Turkey under Presidents Grover Cleveland and William McKinley. Mr. Straus was the first Jew to enter the Cabinet of an American President, as Secretary of the Department of Commerce and Labor under President Theodore Roosevelt.

Although a Republican, Mr. Straus served under two Democratic Presidents, Grover Cleveland and Woodrow Wilson, both of whom appointed him to The Hague Tribunal "as a man versed in government affairs and diplomacy, and possessing a proper quasi-judicial temperament."

In 1912 he ran on the Theodore Roosevelt Progressive Republican ticket for governor of New York. He was not elected, but he had the distinction of pulling more than 397,000 votes, or three thousand more than Roosevelt received as the candidate for President on the same ticket.

Throughout his life Straus was elated over the fact that it was given to him to represent his fellow Jews through all official recognitions bestowed upon him. He was president of the Jewish Publication Society, a member of the executive committee of the American Jewish Committee, and one of the founders of the Young Men's Hebrew Association in New York City in 1884.

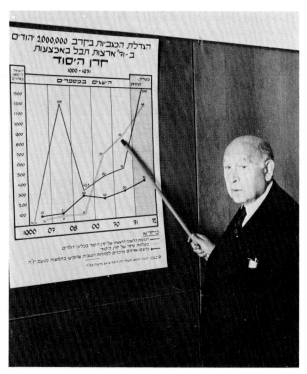

Rabbi Israel Goldstein, a rabbi and a Zionist leader, is now living in Israel where he was world chairman of the Keren Ha-Yesod in raising funds on behalf of Israel in seventy-one countries throughout the world. Rabbi Goldstein also directs a school for boys in Jerusalem and is head of the Jewish National Fund. He is past president of the Jewish Conciliation Court of America and was one of the foremost exponents of Zionism in America, believing that a rebuilt Eretz Israel would bring incalculable benefit to world Jewry and to civilization.

Susan Sontag, young intellectual essayist. She has been called the Mary McCarthy of this generation. Her best known books include *A Trip to Hanoi* and collections of essays examining the cultural scene. Her latest book is *Styles of Radical Will*. She has been published in *Partisan Review, New York Review of Books,* and *Commentary*.

# CHAPTER 12

# Intermarriage—Who Is a Jew?

NAPOLEON, IN QUESTIONING the theologians at Leyden University, asked: "Why are the Jews still here?"

The survival of the Jews as an ethnic group is one of the great phenomenons of world history. Many reasons have been advanced for this phenomenon, but I believe that the basic reason for it lies in the strength of the Jewish family.

For protection from plundering nomads, it became necessary for strangers to gain admission into a family group and for Jewish families in turn to take in unrelated Israelites. Thus appeared the extraordinarily large families of the period of the Biblical Judges. Ordinarily, the head of the family was the patriarch who gave it his name. In ancient times each family had its own religious traditions and its own burial ground. When the family lived together, all goods and especially immovables were common property.

The wife enjoyed a high position in the family. While she never approached the status of her husband, she was called by his name. She participated in the religious functions and ceremonies, could possess property and dispose of it. The woman of the Bible could not divorce her husband, although she could desert him.

In modern times, the Jewish family has generally been an institution of solidarity and stability. Judaism is really a family cult with most of the rituals conducted around the dinner table. "Family, chastity, affection, piety, forbearance, and joyousness" form the base of the pyramid on which the communal life was securely erected.

The father was duty bound to give his son an education, as well as to teach him a handicraft by which he could earn a living. Reciprocally, the child was honor bound to revere both his father and his mother, "for God makes more of it than honor of Himself." The home had its own family feasts and fasts. The Sabbath and the holidays were observed by customs and ceremonies within the family group. There were also special anniversaries of joy and sorrow which each family observed as its individual traditions. There were special dishes prepared for Sabbath, holidays, and special occasions. Distinguished guests would deliver special sermons in the home, and even when the family sat alone, the attempt was made to discuss some learned subject at every meal. Following the Friday evening or Sabbath morning meals, the company would sing table hymns following the grace. All these customs served to bind the members of the family closer. The home was as much a place of religious devotion, study, and reverence as the synagogue.

Many factors in contemporary America have disrupted the uniform pattern of Jewish life. It is enough to say that the breakdown of the stability of the family in general today has had its specific effect on Jewish home life, as it has had on the family life of all other religious groups. But in addition to such general reasons for this as the growth of feminism, the transferring of home functions to institutions, and the secularization of religion, there is the factor of intermarriage. Or perhaps, it is more accurate to say the *problem* of intermarriage. In the 1920s, *Abie's Irish Rose* was a play that dealt with this phenomenon. Its audiences knew that Jews wanted to be Americans and that one of the ways to become American was to marry an Irish girl.

Mr. Arnold Schwartz, research analyst with the American Jewish Committee and a researcher in the sociology of American Judaism at the City University of New York, predicts a continuing rise in intermarriage between Jew and Gentile. Mr. Schwartz's predictions appear in an article recently published in the *American Jewish Yearbook*. At the present writing between 10 and 15 per cent of all Jews in the United States who marry, marry a non-Jew.

This rate will increase, if not precipitously, at least appreciably because Jews have entered the mainstream of American life. Jewish rye bread is a staple on the American dining table, and the school board these days insists on shlepping the sixth grade to all the cathedrals, churches, and synagogues in town to prove that all men are brothers.

Another sociological factor is that the Jewish merchant will not marry the daughter or the sister of his Gentile merchant colleague. He will marry a sales girl, whose father is a mill worker. The Jewish lawyer will not marry the sister or the daughter of his Gentile colleague in the courts. He, too, will marry the girl who works in his office, whose father may be a barber.

In all such marriages, the Gentile girl achieves a higher economic status than that she came from. In other words, the Jew must bring something in addition to himself to the union. In those marriages involving a Jewish male and a Gentile female, the Jew is usually self-sustaining by career. That is, a Gentile girl must be able to say to herself or to her friends, "I married a Jew, but he's rich," or "he's a writer," or "he's a college professor," etc.

I do not think these insights throw any light on the Jewish girl who marries a Gentile. It may be simplistic, but I think the reason for this is that when a woman marries, legally she changes her name. If Edith OBrien goes to mass as Mrs. Joseph Goldberg, she is often considered an anomaly. If Edith Goldberg goes to shul as Mrs. John Daley, she is not, possibly because the Jewish religious law defines a Jew as one whose mother is a Jew. If she goes to mass with John Daley, her sister Catholics will think this a perfectly natural metamorphosis.

In recent years much of the antagonism within the Jewish community toward the Gentile spouse has disappeared. The non-Jewish female often enters the synagogue and participates in all its functions. At one time in a North Carolina town, the only Jewish home that kept kosher was that of a Gentile wife.

Recently *Look* magazine, before it closed shop, ran an article about intermarriage between Gentile and Jew. It indicated that Judaism may be losing 70 per cent of the children born to mixed couples. There are Jews who are worried about this. But it is not a new worry.

When Napoleon opened the ghettos of Europe in 1807, there were rabbis who bewailed the vanishing Jews who would be swallowed up by the Gentile society.

But the Jew did not vanish after 1807, nor after 1910, nor will he vanish after 1972 nor after 2072.

But *Look* magazine does not fret alone. The Commission on Jewish Affairs of the American Jewish Congress recently sponsored a conference on intermarriage between Gentile and Jew.

At the conference, Rabbi Leo Jung of the Jewish Center in New York said: "Intermarriage . . . is unfair to the Jewish people, past, present, and future; it is unfair to the non-Jew; it is unfair to the institution of marriage."

Rabbi Joseph Klein of Temple Emanuel in Worcester, Massachusetts, said: "Most Jewish parents, even those who are lax in their religious observance, regard the marriage of their child to a non-Jew as a calamity . . . they are completely beaten in their arguments if there is a rabbi in the community who is known to solemnize mixed marriages."

Rabbi David Eichhorn of the National Jewish Welfare Board said: "We shall need the forbearance of Moses, the wisdom of Solomon, and the patience of Job to solve all the problems that have come upon us and will continue to come upon us because of the gradually increasing number of religiously mixed marriages in the United States of America."

To this last, I must say "God help us," because Moses, Solomon, and Job have apparently thrown the situation in our lap.

To Rabbi Klein, let me say that there are always parents who exert pressures to prevent marriages, mixed or not. Wise children pay no attention. Nothing calms parents and dignifies them like a grandchild.

As to Rabbi Jung, I say he certainly has placed a heavy burden on the young who marry, whether they marry Gentiles or Jews. Does *anyone take* a mate with the idea of playing fair with the past, present, and future of the Jews?

We Jews, no more than anyone else, cannot have it both ways. We cannot live in a pluralistic society with the guarantees of religious freedom and keep inviolate all our religious traditions and mores.

What has always made me smile is my observation of the paradox of the many Jews who wage desperate war to join the Gentile country club and at the same time insist that other Jews not marry Gentiles.

What I think everyone misses in the dialogue on mixed marriages (although Rabbi Klein seems somewhat aware of it) is that religious ritual itself is not enough to insure absolute genetic perpetuity.

A corollary to the questions of Jewish survival and Jewish family survival is the problem of "who is a Jew?"

Few Christians were worried lest the Dead Sea Scrolls refute some basic tenet of the faith. The *idea* is the important thing.

By the same token there was hardly a single protest when scholars changed the name of the Red Sea through which Moses led the children of Israel to the Sea of Reeds. No one was disturbed. It makes no difference. The *idea* is all that matters. The Idea of Judaism also is eternal.

Look at the new modern religion—communism. It has millions of adherents in Russia and China. Yet an ordinary speech by a middle-ranking Party functionary can shake its whole foundation and the people start tearing plaques off the walls, cease venerating old leaders, change the names of streets and cities, and pull down statues.

But the Judaic-Christian civilization exists in time and not in space, and does not depend on the success of the next "Five-Year Plan."

The amazing irony is that the question of who is a Jew is really decided, finally, by the vast Christian majority. I knew a little boy whose father was a Jew and his mother a Christian. He got his first black eye in a fight with a kid who called him "a Jew" the week after he made his first Communion in the Roman Catholic Church.

But the trouble with considering an anti-Semite's definition, however, is that it does not apply to the here-and-now. Nor does it really even apply to people. For the anti-Semite refuses to see the Jew as a brother human.

There is another definition of the Jew in modern literature. The great novel of the twentieth century is James Joyce's *Ulysses*, whose hero is a Jew who lives in Dublin and is named Leopold Bloom. Joyce chose a Jew as a hero because he wanted a "wanderer" to typify the modern Odysseus. Writers consider the Jew as a symbol of the aberrant man of culture to whom the world has denied a forum. The use of the Jew as a symbol animates much of modern literature because of the temptation to portray him as a modern Everyman, a figure possessed of moral strength but handicapped by other circumstances. For this symbol is indicative of what most novelists want to talk about—the dilemma of cultural estrangement, of homelessness, of loneliness.

This definition of a Jew is not a logical or working definition at all.

But there is a novelist who has come close to a working definition. Curiously, he is Arthur Miller, the Pulitzer prize winning playwright whose first work was a novel called *Focus* which described a Christian named Miller who "looked" Jewish and moved into a neighborhood where he was "accused" of being Jewish. He fought this, but no one really believed him, and in the end he resigned himself to suffering as a Jew for no reason other than the fact that Jews suffer. Bernard Malamud's fine novel *The Assistant* makes the same point about an Italian thief who falls in love with a Jewish girl.

Malamud and Miller have hit upon a philosophic truth. And in the last analysis, it is the sectarian philosophers who furnish the definition of a Jew that we seek and need. Jean-Paul Sartre, the French existentialist, says quite simply, "A Jew is a man other men call a Jew." This definition will serve. But Professor Sidney Hook offers an even more satisfying definition in his essay, "Reflections on the Jewish Question, which appears in *Mid-Century* (ed. by Harold Ribalow, Beechhurst Press, N.Y., 1955)." He says, "A Jew is anyone who for any reason calls himself or is called such in any community whose practice makes note of the distinction."

I was sitting in the lounge of a jet plane returning home from Israel not too long ago, and I chanced into a discussion with a great philanthropist. He is an American-born Jew who has devoted his time, energies, and a good portion of his wealth to Israeli charities. Something about Israel, however, dismays him. He told me sadly, "They don't go to shul. I've never seen anything like it. They don't go to shul."

I told the philanthropist not to burden his heart with worry about the Israeli non-shul-goers. After all, there is a difference between him and the Israeli. The philanthropist lives in a suburb and when he rises in the morning he *needs* identity, for the philanthropist's banker does not consider him simply a suburban developer. At the luncheon table in the City Club, his banker says to his friends, "I have some of the best Jewish business in town." Nor does his lawyer consider him simply a client who is a graduate engineer turned land developer. His lawyer tells colleagues during a bull session at the convention in Honolulu, "Our office has been getting most of the Jewish business in recent years."

My philanthropist thus needs to confirm for himself his identity as a Jew that others thrust strongly upon him. Because of the social segregation which sets in after sundown each day, he needs to pile one activity atop the other until the temple becomes the center of his sociological being. Thus, he creates the illusion that this kind of activity is the basis of being a Jew.

I visited with the late Bernard M. Baruch three or four times. "Does he go to shul?" people asked me, as though somehow Baruch would cease being Jewish if he didn't. Invariably, the fellow who asks "Does Baruch go to shul?" attends shul himself perhaps three times a year. But he needs Baruch in the shul every Sabbath to add greater dignity to his identity. So too does he need the Israeli to go to shul—more so, in fact. But the Israeli is already in shul. When he gets up in the morning he has no compulsion to prove anything nor does he need to pride himself on this. They have deserts to irrigate and borders to patrol and trees to plant. The whole country is a shul.

The Israelis, in short, aren't troubled by identity problems; they know what they are. Businessmen are simply businessmen in Israel and writers are writers. Only the rest of the world is populated by businessmen and Jewish businessmen and has books that are written by writers and Jewish writers.

There are those who are secure in their Jewishness who never worry whether Bernard Baruch went to shul or not.

They also do not worry about "the vanishing American Jew."

But let us not minimize the importance of our ace-in-the-hole —the Christians. The Christians dare not let us vanish. We are the "living witnesses." The Roman Catholic burial service, ". . . into the bosom of Abraham," would have no meaning if there were no Jews, and the Protestants look forward to the Biblical fulfillment: "Ten men out of all languages of the nations shall take hold of the hem of him that is a Jew, saying, we will go with you, for we have heard God is with you."

Without us there can be no Second Coming of Jesus.

An assistant to Reverend Billy Graham in a bantering mood asked me to become a Christian. I told him no, because the men who have most to do with the intellectual development of man— Jesus, Karl Marx, Sigmund Freud and Albert Einstein—were all Jews and that's too much of a heritage for me to give up.

CHAPTER 13

# The Amazing City

NEW YORK CITY is even getting slams these days from out-of-state senators. They say New York City is dirtier than some of the towns back home.

New York's problem is that it represents all the woes of the urban twentieth century in microcosm. Twenty-six thousand tons of garbage can pile up every day on the streets. A girl with a forty-eight-inch bust starts a panic on Wall Street at noon hour. Police commissioners leaving office don't even give the mayor two weeks notice. The neighborhoods are constantly besieging the schools. The middle class who need the city for their working hours have deserted it for their neat bungalows in the suburbs.

Despite all, the city survives and one of the reasons it survives is that if you want to make it big, New York is the city where you make it the biggest.

San Francisco was kind to Allen Ginsberg, Chicago to Carl Sandburg, Paris to F. Scott Fitzgerald and Ernest Hemingway and London to T. S. Eliot. But New York made Arthur Miller, Norman Mailer, Richard Rodgers, Leonard Bernstein, and Barbara Streisand. It has the only theater in the United States and while the theater is always at a low ebb, its present low ebb is running a lot higher than Hollywood's, which once had more money and more resources.

It was the city to which the Germans, the Irish, the Jews, the Italians, and the Poles came, and now come the Negroes and the Puerto Ricans. Not all of them made it big, but a sufficient number did. The descendents of the immigrants still think that if you

The Greatest Jewish City in the World.

are going to make it big, make it big in New York. After Alfred E. Smith lost the presidential election to Herbert Hoover in 1928, he helped build the Empire State Building.

Over the past decades, I have had dozens of friends who deserted the city, who left Columbia University for Antioch, who left the *Post* to work in Toledo, who left the theater and the city for a job selecting films for an airlines company. I myself left for Charlotte. Like William Butler Yeats's Byzantium, New York is no city for old men.

But the sons of these men return to the Big City to seek a more adventurous fortune than they might find elsewhere. Until this hope evaporates, there is still every chance that New York will someday prove the most successful experiment in urban living ever conceived.

Thus the Greatest Jewish City in the world.

But New York is not only the greatest Jewish City in the world, it is also a great Irish city and a great Polish city and the greatest Negro city and a great Italian city and the greatest German city outside of Europe and a great Puerto Rican city. And while all these groups may not be struggling to become good neighbors, they are not advocating a neighborhood nationalism. They may still be remote from one another, not responsive to one another's needs, but they are no more remote than members of the Common Market in Europe.

There is a common interest that one day the citizens of this city will realize serves all their needs as New York indeed serves the interest of millions of Americans who live outside it. It is still the magnetic city, still the city to which the young trek from the heartland. They still believe it will work, that their ambitions will find fulfillment in diversity, their hopes filled by differences become material, their journey still motivated by the willingness to see the alien and recognize it as their own.

BECAUSE IF IT DOES NOT WORK IN NEW YORK, IT WILL WORK NOWHERE.

During the traditional Passover seder, the family repeats the prayer "Dayyenu" (it would have been enough for us):

> Had he brought us out of Egypt, and
> not divided the sea from us—Dayennu.

Had he divided the sea, and not
permitted us to cross on dry land—Dayyenu.

Had he permitted us to cross the sea on
dry land, and not sustained us for forty
years in the desert—Dayyenu.

Thus the Jews in America and especially of New York could paraphrase the traditional Passover prayer:

We crossed the ocean in
steerage but we were on the way to America—Dayyenu.

We did not find the streets paved with gold—Dayyenu.

We found the sweat shops
miserable and the tenements full
of roaches, but we were now in a land
where we could freely worship God and
freely express ourselves—Dayyenu.

# Appendix

WE INCLUDE in this appendix a *partial* listing of Jewish organizations and associations in New York City, prefaced here by some well-chosen words from one of America's leading Jews:

"If any one impulse can be said to be commonly characteristic of Jews, it is devotion to charity. This impulse is deeply grounded in ancient religious traditions, which placed the highest premium on charity and lovingkindness in the hierarchy of values that make up the Jewish way of life. It is well illustrated by the following quotation from the Midrash, a collection of commentaries on the biblical text:

> In the future world, a man will be asked, 'What was your occupation?' If he reply, 'I fed the hungry,' then the reply is, 'This is the gate of the Lord; he who feeds the hungry, let him enter.'
>
> So too with giving drink to the thirsty, clothing the naked, sheltering the homeless, with those who look after orphans, and with those generally who do deeds of lovingkindness. All these are gates of the Lord, and those who do such deeds shall enter within them.

"The catalogue of American Jewish welfare is endless. The American Red Cross was organized in Washington, D.C., home of Adolphus S. Solomons. Julius Rosenwald of Chicago established a $30 million fund for Negro welfare and education as part of his lifetime contribution of $70 million to charity. The three Straus brothers of New York Isidor, Nathan and Oscar were almost as generous. They built hospitals and tuberculosis sanitariums, set up relief stations that dispensed more than a million meals during the depression winter of 1914–15, led the fight for the pasteurization of New York City's milk supply and helped build a Roman Catholic Church. And then there is the Guggenheim family, of course, who set up a foundation which since 1925 has given educational fellowships to thousands of artists, writers, scholars and scientists.

"Hundreds of institutions for human welfare scattered over the nation are Jewish in creation and Jewish in support, although the bulk of the beneficiaries are non-Jewish. In its early days the Henry Street Settlement in New York, which was founded by Lillian D. Wald and financed by Jacob H. Schiff, became a world model for creative social work and was the cradle of the visiting nurse service.

"Another Jewish innovation is the Council of Jewish Federations and Welfare Funds, an association of community organizations which coordinates the many national and international appeals (such as the energetic United Jewish Appeal for overseas aid) and analyzes the needs and finances of each.

"Jewish women have been especially vigorous in welfare and civic work. Hadassah, one of the most influential women's organizations, is particularly active in Israel. Another leading group, the B'nai B'rith women, with chapters throughout the United States, is busily engaged in civic, charitable and humanitarian affairs, and works closely in coordination with the ADL in the area of civil rights."—Dore Schary*

## Community, Defense,

## and Human Relations Agencies†

American Jewish Committee, 164 East 56th Street, New York

American Jewish Congress, 15 East 84th Street, New York

Anti-Defamation League of B'nai B'rith, 315 Lexington Avenue, New York

Commission on Social Action of Reform Judaism, 838 Fifth Avenue, New York

Jewish Labor Committee, 25 East 78th Street, New York

Jewish War Veterans of the United States of America, 276 Fifth Avenue, New York

---

* From "What Is the American Jew?" by Dore Schary, in *Image of the Jews: Teachers' Guide to Jews and Their Religion,* published by Anti-Defamation League, New York, 1970. Quoted with permission.

† Partial listing of Jewish organizations and associations in New York City, courtesy Seymour P. Lachman and officers of the Anti-Defamation League. For further listing see American Jewish Yearbook and American Jewish Organizations Directory.

## Cultural

American Academy for Jewish Research, 3080 Broadway, New York

American Biblical Encyclopedia Society, 210 West 91st Street, New York

American Jewish Historical Society, 150 Fifth Avenue, New York

Conference on Jewish Social Studies, Inc., 2629 Broadway, New York

Hebrew Arts School for Music and Dance, 120 West 16th Street, New York

Histadruth Ivruth of America, Inc., 120 West 16th Street, New York

Jewish Book Council of America, 15 East 26th Street, New York

Jewish Information Bureau, 250 West 57th Street, New York

Leo Baeck Institute, Inc., 129 East 73rd Street, New York

National Foundation for Jewish Culture, 122 East 42nd Street, New York

National Hebrew Culture Council, 1776 Broadway, New York

National Jewish Music Council, 15 East 26th Street, New York

Yivo Institute for Jewish Research, 1048 Fifth Avenue, New York

## Education

American Association for Jewish Education, 101 Fifth Avenue, New York

B'nai B'rith Hillel Foundation, 2901 Campus Road, Brooklyn, New York

B'nai B'rith Youth Organization, 315 Lexington Avenue, New York

Commission on Jewish Education of Central Conference of American Rabbis, 838 Fifth Avenue, New York

Herzliah Hebrew Teachers Institute, 69 Bank Street, New York

Jewish Educaion Commitee of New York, Inc., 426 West 58th Street, New York

Jewish Teachers Seminary and People's University, 69 Bank Street, New York

National Academy for Adult Jewish Studies, 218 E. 70th St., New York

National Conference of Synagogue Youth, 84 Fifth Avenue, New York

National Council for Jewish Education, 101 Fifth Avenue, New York

National Council of Beth Jacob Schools, 125 Heyward Street, Brooklyn, New York

National Federation of Hebrew Teachers and Principals, 120 West 16th Street, New York

Sholom Aleichem Folk Institute, Inc., 41 Union Square, New York

Teachers Institute-Seminary College of Jewish Studies, 3080 Broadway, New York

Torah Umesorah—National Society for Hebrew Day Schools, 156 Fifth Avenue, New York

Yavneh, National Religious Jewish Students Association, 84 Fifth Avenue, New York

## Federations and Funds

American Jewish Joint Distribution Committee (JDC), 60 East 42nd Street, New York

Council of Jewish Federations and Welfare Funds, Inc., 315 Park Avenue South, New York

Federation of Jewish Philanthropies of New York, 130 East 59th Street, New York

United Jewish Appeal of Greater New York, Inc., 220 West 58th Street, New York

## Fraternal and Social Welfare

Bnai Zion (The American Fraternal Zionist Organization), 50 West 57th Street, New York

B'nai B'rith Foundation of the United States, 315 Lexington Avenue, New York

Farband–Labor Zionist Order, 575 Sixth Avenue, New York

Jewish Agricultural Society, Inc., 386 Park Avenue South, New York

National Conference of Jewish Communal Service, 15 East 26th Street, New York

National Council of Jewish Women, Inc., 1 West 47th Street, New York

Sephardic Jewish Brotherhood of America, Inc., 116 East 169th Street, Bronx, New York

United HIAS Service, Inc., 200 Park Avenue South, New York

Workmen's Circle, 175 East Broadway, New York

World Federation of YMHAS and Jewish Community Centers, 145 East 32nd Street, New York

## Libraries

City College, Davidson Collection of Judaica of The Morris Raphael Cohen Library, Convent Avenue and 135th Street

Hebrew Union College—Jewish Institute of Religion, 40 West 68th Street, New York

Jewish Division, New York Public Library, Fifth Avenue and 42nd Street, New York

Jewish Theological Seminary of America, 3080 Broadway, New York

Columbia University Judaic Collection of the Nicholas Murray Butler Library, Broadway and 116th Street, New York

New York University, Jewish Culture Foundation, 2 Washington Square North, New York

Yeshiva University, 500 West 185th Street, New York

Yivo Institute for Jewish Research, 1048 Fifth Avenue, New York

Zionist Archives and Library, 515 Park Avenue, New York

## Museums and Exhibits

House of Living Judaism—Berg Memorial, 838 Fifth Avenue, New York

Jewish Museum, 1109 Fifth Avenue, New York

Jewish Theological Seminary of America, 3080 Broadway, New York

## Seminaries and Religious Organizations

### ORTHODOX:

Agudath Israel of America, 5 Beekman Street, New York

American Conference of Cantors, 40 West 68th Street, New York

Cantors Assembly of America, 150 Fifth Avenue, New York

Jewish Reconstructionist Foundation, 15 West 86th Street, New York

Mesivta Rabbi Chaim Berlin Rabbinical Academy, 1593 Coney Island Avenue, Brooklyn, New York

National Council of Young Israel, 3 West 16th Street, New York

Rabbinical Council of America, 220 Park Avenue South, New York

Union of Orthodox Jewish Congregations of America, 84 Fifth Avenue, New York

Union of Orthodox Rabbis of the United States and Canada, Inc., 235 East Broadway, New York

United Lubavitcher Yeshivoth, 843 Ocean Parkway, Brooklyn, New York

Yeshiva Torah Vodaath and Mesivta (Rabbinical Seminary), 425 East 9th Street, Brooklyn, New York

Yeshiva University, 500 West 185th Street, New York

### CONSERVATIVE:

Jewish Theological Seminary of America, 3080 Broadway, New York

Rabbinical Assembly of America, 3080 Broadway, New York

### REFORM:

Central Conference of American Rabbis, 790 Madison Avenue, New York

Hebrew Union College—Jewish Institute of Religion, 40 West 68th Street, New York

Union of American Hebrew Congregations, 838 Fifth Avenue, New York

## Theater, Music and Arts

Educational Alliance, 197 East Broadway, New York

Folksbiene Playhouse, 175 East Broadway, New York

Joan of Arc Community Center, 154 West 93rd Street, New York

Theodor Herzl Institute, 515 Park Avenue, New York

YM–YWHA, Lexington Avenue and 92nd Street, New York

## Youth Organizations

National Conference of Synagogue Youth of The Union of Orthodox Jewish Congregations of America, 84 Fifth Avenue, New York

National Council of Young Israel, 3 West 16th Street, New York

National Jewish Welfare Board, 15 East 26th Street, New York

United Synagogue Youth (USY), 218 East 70th Street, New York

Young Judaea, 116 West 14th Street, New York

## Zionist and American-Culture Organizations

America-Israel Cultural Foundation, 4 East 54th Street, New York

American Committee for Boys Town Jerusalem, 8 W. 40th Street, New York

American Committee for the Weizmann Institute of Science, 515 Park Avenue, New York

American Zionist Youth Council, 515 Park Avenue, New York

Hadassah, The Women's Zionist Organization of America, Inc., 65 East 52nd Street, New York

Hebrew University—Technion Joint Maintenance Appeal, 11 East 69th Street, New York

Jewish Agency—American Section, Inc., 515 Park Avenue, New York

Labor Zionist Movement, 200 Park Avenue South, New York

Mizrachi-Hapoel Hamizrachi, 200 Park Avenue South, New York

Mizrachi Women's Organization of America, 242 Park Avenue South, New York

State of Israel (Bonds Corporation), 215 Park Avenue South, New York

Student Zionist Organization, 515 Park Avenue, New York

Zionist Organization of America, 145 E. 32nd Street, New York

## Civil Service Organizations

Akiba (Board of Education)

Association of Jewish Employees (Department of Social Services, Welfare)

Association of Jewish Court Attaches

Association of Jewish State Employees

Avir Naki (Department of Air Pollution Control)

Briyuth (Department of Health)

Emeth (Department of Law)

Gibborim (Department of Correction)

Gonen (Transit Police)

Habonim (Department of Public Works)

Habonim (Department of Buildings)

Hebrew Spiritual Society

Jewish Postal Workers Welfare League

Knyoth (Department of Purchase)

Morim, Jewish Teachers Association

Naer Tormid (Fire Department)

Ormyim (Department of Water Supply, Gas, and Electricity)

Rofeh (Department of Hospitals)

Sabbath Observers in Civil Service

Sholom (Transit Authority)

Shomrim (Police Department)

Shotrim (Housing Police)

Sofrim (Comptroller, Finance)